Instant Pot Cookbook

Quick and Easy Traditional Indian Recipes for Everyday Eating

ABOUT THE AUTHOR

The goal of "Lady Pannana" Publishing Company is to provide you with easy-to-cook, authentic, and tasty recipes.

To increase your health, energy, and well-being, Lady Pannana cookbooks bring together the best of international cuisines and teach you how to cook them in the comfort of your own home.

From special diets to international treats, pick up a cookbook today and lose yourself in a whole new world of possibilities.

No mealtime should be boring, so go ahead and treat yourself!

Browse our catalog of titles and don't forget to tell us what you think about our books. We want to create a better experience for our readers. Your voice, your opinion, and your input only serve to ensure that the next time you pick up a Lady Pannana Publishing Title, it will be better than the last!

To find out more about Healthy Cooking and Recipes visit our blog below

Visit Our Blog => ladypannana.com

You can also stay up-to-date with what's going on here by subscribing for free updates, liking Lady Pannana on FaceBook, or following us on Instagram, Twitter etc.

FaceBook: ladypannana.com/facebook

Twitter: ladypannana.com/twitter

Instagram: ladypannana.com/instagram

Pinterest: ladypannana.com/pinterest

Tumbler: ladypannana.com/tumblr

Google+: ladypannana.com/google

YouTube: ladypannana.com/youtube

LinkedIn: ladypannana.com/linkedin

Visit **our author page** on Amazon to see other work done by Lady Pannana.

ladypannana.com/amazonauthor

If you have any questions or suggestions feel free to contact us at

ladypannana@gmail.com

Thank you for taking the time to read this and we look forward to seeing you on the blog sometime soon!

Cheers,

Lady Pannana

Wait! Before You Continue... Would You Like to Get Healthier, Happier and Enjoy Eating at the Same Time?

Would You Like to Increase Your Overall Well-Being?

If you answered YES, you are not alone. We believe almost everyone wants to have a good body and be healthy by simply start eating clean and diet. Unfortunately, most of us have no idea how to do it. Yes, dieting can work, but starving yourself just leads to frustration and failure. Also, dieting will not help your health! It will just harm you. What we recommend you here it isn't dieting, it is a LIFESTYLE!

Right now, you can get full **FREE access to Low-Carb** eBook+Paleo Report to Learn How to Cook Tasty and More Important HEALTHY Recipes,

so you can easily and quickly start pursuing your goals.

Low - carb eating is something that has become increasingly popular in recent years. It has been linked with a range of health benefits including:

- Improved weight loss (even when you're not consciously restricting your calories).
- Improved concentration.
- Increased energy levels.
- Prevention and treatment of various chronic diseases.
- Reduced blood glucose levels (which are particularly beneficial for diabetics).
- Reduced blood pressure.

Free Bonus

Go Here to Get Instant Access

ladypannana.com/freebook

Medical Disclaimer

Table of Content

Introduction

I want to thank you and congratulate you for downloading the book, "*Instant Pot Cookbook: Indian Traditional, Quick and Easy Recipes for Everyday Eating.*"

We all want to enjoy good food, for which we find ourselves exploring various cuisines in search of that tantalizing taste. One cuisine that often stands out is Indian cuisine. This is because of its avalanche of flavors. Indian cuisine does something few cuisines can successfully do. It provides sweet, spicy, sour, and hot flavors all at one go. This palette of flavors leaves your tongue tingling for more. Unfortunately, the exotic ingredients and unfamiliar sounding dishes that make up the basis of Indian cuisine may intimidate you. Picture this. Indian cuisine regularly uses 20 to 30 spices in various dishes. If you're used to the usual 1 or 2 spices, the thought of incorporating all those spices in your cooking may indeed be overwhelming.

However, you don't have to be intimidated by all the spices you will be using. Here's why. Each spice has its purpose. Apart from bringing with them many health benefits, spices also add excitement and flavor to your meals. The spices and sauces in Indian cuisine make bland food come alive. They also give you the freedom to be both creative and adventurous. Sounds great, right?

Unfortunately, preparing exciting Indian meals often means spending long hours in the kitchen and checking the food from time to time to make sure it does not burn or overcook. This may make you reserve traditional Indian dishes for special occasions, instead of enjoying them every day. But that does not have to be the case. You can still enjoy a variety of Indian dishes without expending too much energy or spending too much time in the kitchen. This is possible thanks to the Instant Pot. And thanks to this book, you will learn how to prepare finger-licking Indian recipes with an Instant Pot.

In this book, you will learn:

- The benefits of using an Instant Pot

- Some helpful tips to make using the Instant Pot easier

- Tasty Indian recipes you can prepare in your Instant Pot

After reading this book, you will have no reason not to make Indian meals a part of your everyday cooking, especially because the Instant Pot makes the process very fast and easy. That said, you might want to adjust the amount of spices that are recommended in this book's recipes after you cook your first or second dish and notice that the food is too spicy. This is because Indian foods tend to be really spicy and sometimes that makes them unbearable for anyone who is not used to too much spice in food. However, if you don't find them too spicy, feel free to use them as they are. Flexibility is the name of the game.

If you are excited about making your debut into Indian meals with an Instant Pot, this book will hold you by the hand to make sure your experience will be as smooth as possible. Let's begin.

Thanks again for purchasing this book. I hope you enjoy it!

Before we discuss how to prepare delicious Indian meals with an Instant Pot, let's start by understanding why you should make the Instant Pot your preferred cooking appliance whether you are cooking Indian meals or not.

Chapter 1: Why The Instant Pot?

Well, this has something to do with the very nature of Indian cuisine. Here's the thing. Many traditional Indian dishes can take hours to prepare. This usually means using various cooking pots and checking the food from time to time to make sure it does not burn or overcook. The Instant Pot, which is a new-generation pressure cooker, eliminates the need for this. First, this electric pressure cooker uses 70% less energy and cooks the food 2 to 6 times faster. But there are other reasons to use the Instant Pot to prepare Indian dishes. These include:

1. Safety

Safety is always an issue whenever a traditional pressure cooker is concerned. It's difficult to forget tales of mishaps people used to narrate about such pressure cookers. But you don't need to worry about safety as far as the Instant Pot is concerned. It is fitted with 10 built-in safety mechanisms. These mechanisms make sure that explosions and issues such as steamy rattling do not occur. As long as you follow the right procedures, especially when opening the lid after cooking, you'll have no safety issues with your Instant Pot.

2. Multi-Function

The Instant Pot was created to perform up to seven functions. It is a multi-use electric pressure cooker. It is also a rice cooker, slow cooker, steamer, and yogurt maker. You can also use it as a warming pot and as a sauté and browning pan. All these functions make your work easier, as you don't have to purchase and use various cooking pots and other appliances just to cook your meals. You can actually cut back on the appliances you use. This also saves time when it comes to cleaning.

3. Ease of Use

Another good thing about the Instant Pot is that it is easy to use. The buttons are well labeled. Once you familiarize yourself with them, your work will be easy indeed. You'll find yourself mostly using the 'Sauté', 'Manual' and the '+' and '-' buttons. These buttons will allow you to select the cooking option and set the time. If you are a new cook, you'll have fun learning to prepare various dishes using the Instant Pot. All you have to do is to follow the recipe, press the appropriate buttons, and wait for the food to cook.

4. Convenience

The Instant Pot is convenient to use. Most importantly, it is fully automated. This means you don't need to keep an eye on the timer or adjust the heat. The Instant Pot will do all these for you. Once you place your food inside and set the time, you can go on with your day. Once the food is ready, your Instant Pot will switch to the 'Keep Warm' mode: this will keep your food warm for up to 10 hours. Another good thing about the Instant Pot is the delayed cooking time option. You can set it to cook up to 24 hours later, if you wish. This makes it easier to prepare your ingredients beforehand and plan your meals ahead.

5. No Need to Defrost

It's not unusual to come home after working the whole day and realize you forgot to remove something from the freezer. This normally forces you to use a microwave to quickly thaw the food before you can cook it. This is not necessary when you have the Instant Pot. The Instant Pot gives you the freedom to cook your food without thawing it or defrosting it first. All you have to do is just to place your food in the Instant Pot and let the food cook as it usually does. This is very convenient indeed.

As you have learned, various benefits come with using the Instant Pot. However, the best part is the numerous recipes you can actually cook using this electric pressure cooker. Let us learn more about what to expect with Indian recipes in the next chapter.

Chapter 2: What Should You Expect Of Indian Cuisine?

You should expect diversity, as Indian cuisine is vast. It encompasses all the cuisines native to India plus all the cuisines borrowed from other regions. This means that it has been influenced by factors such as climate, culture, occupations, ethnicity, and other matters, such as soil types which impact the fruits, vegetables, spices, and herbs grown in the country.

But there are certain staples you can expect to come across. These include foods, such as rice, pearl millet, and whole-wheat flour. Indian cuisine also makes good use of a variety of lentils. When following an Indian cuisine, you can expect to eat foods such as mung beans, split lentils, red lentils, urad, pigeon peas, kidney beans, chickpeas, and black-eyed peas.

What about the spices?

Indisputably, Indian cuisine uses plenty of spices. Some of the spices and flavorings you can expect include garlic, black mustard seed, ginger, coriander, turmeric, chili pepper, cardamom, hing or asafoetida (also spelled without an "o" as asafetida), and cumin. You can also expect to use garam masala, which is a spice that is usually made by blending 5 or more dried spices. Usually, these spices include clove, cinnamon, and cardamom. Many cooks make their own blend and you can experiment with the same.

Apart from the various spices, some leaves are often used for flavoring. These include coriander leaves, mint leaves, bay leaves, curry leaves, and fenugreek leaves. The trick is to know which spices go well with others. You can only know this by practically testing the mixtures. Essence such as rose petal, cardamom, nutmeg, and saffron are often used to season sweet dishes.

Before we look at the recipes, it is important to mention that you will come across the word 'tempering' several times. So what exactly is tempering? Tempering entails cooking whole spices such as cumin, mustard seeds, and dried chilies among others in ghee, butter, or oil for some time to enhance flavor. As you will learn from the recipes later, you temper when you start cooking and then add the other ingredients. This should not scare you though. As you embark on trying out various Indian Instant Pot dishes, don't be afraid to experiment with various spices.

The subsequent chapters will focus on various Indian recipes you can try out in your Instant Pot. We will start with curries. As you are aware, curries form a major part of Indian cuisine and the various curries you can make are quite diverse. Let us look at some of the curries you can prepare.

Note:

If you don't understand the different Indian words, you may find the recipes a bit hard to understand. That's why each chapter will have a small section at the beginning that discusses the meaning of different words that you can refer to whenever you don't understand a recipe. Explanations for terms that appear in multiple chapters will be repeated to make it easy for you read the book and follow the recipes.

Chapter 3: Instant Pot Curry Recipes

Glossary Of Terms You Will Find In This Chapter

Garam masala: A combination of ground spices that are blended together.

Kasuri methi: A semi-arid crop that is cultivated worldwide. Its leaves consist of three tiny obviate to almost oblong leaflets. Indians usually use its seeds in their ingredients and that is exactly what you should use in this recipe.

Lauki: A Hindi word that stands for a bottle gourd.

Naan: A type of leavened bread that looks like pita bread. It is made with wheat flour and baked in a tandoori oven. It is usually somewhat triangular in shape and forms crispy spots, which come from bubbles that form in the hot clay oven.

Roti: An Indian name for a flat round bread that is normally cooked on a griddle.

Indian Chicken Curry

Servings: 6

Ingredients

3 pounds of chicken thighs or drumsticks, bone-in

¼ cup of cilantro, chopped

2 tablespoons of cashew paste

1 ½ teaspoons of garam masala

½ cup of water or chicken broth

2 cups of potatoes, cut into 1 ½ inch cubes

1 ½ teaspoons of salt

¾ teaspoon of cayenne or Indian chili powder

¾ teaspoon of ground black pepper

¾ teaspoons of turmeric powder

1 ½ tablespoons of coriander powder

2 tablespoons of tomato paste

1 tablespoon of minced ginger

1 tablespoon of minced garlic

2 cups of finely chopped onions

½ teaspoon of cumin seeds

2-inch of cinnamon stick

1 large bay leaf

3 tablespoons of ghee, butter, or oil

Directions

1. Select the Sauté mode and allow your Instant Pot to heat up. Melt the butter, add in cumin seeds, cinnamon, and bay leaf. Stir the ingredients until fragrant and make sure they do not burn.

2. Add in the onions, ginger, and garlic. Let them cook for about 7 minutes or until golden brown.

3. Mix 2 tablespoons of water and tomato paste and then stir the mixture into the ingredients in your Instant Pot. Cook for 3 minutes or until the tomato paste is cooked. You can add 1 to 2 tablespoons of water, if the ingredients are sticking to your Instant Pot's bottom.

4. Turn off your Instant Pot to prevent the spices from burning. Add in the turmeric, cayenne, coriander, and salt. Stir the mixture frequently until fragrant.

5. Press the Sauté mode again and add in the chicken pieces. Stir the mixture to coat the chicken pieces well.

6. Add ½ cup of chicken broth or water and select the 'Poultry' mode. Set the time for 15 minutes and make sure the valve is in the Sealing position. Once cooking is done, proceed to do a quick release.

7. Blend together 1/3 to ¼ cup of cashews with some water to make cashew paste. If for some reason you can't get cashew paste, you can use coconut cream or heavy cream of cashew butter in place of cashew paste.

8. Add the cashew paste to the chicken curry and stir while in the Sauté mode.

9. Turn off your Instant Pot and proceed to sprinkle some cilantro on top of the chicken curry.

10. Serve with bread, naan, or basmati rice.

Instant Pot Lamb Curry

Servings: 6

Ingredients

1 ½ pounds of cubed lamb stew meat (you can opt for beef or chicken)

1 medium zucchini, diced

3 medium carrots, sliced

1 medium onion, diced

¾ teaspoon of turmeric (omit if using curry powder)

1 ½ tablespoons of garam masala (you may substitute yellow curry powder)

1 (14 oz.) can of diced tomatoes

1 tablespoon of ghee, butter, or oil

A pinch of black pepper to taste

¼ teaspoon sea salt to taste

½ lime juice

½ cup coconut milk

1-inch piece fresh ginger, grated

4 cloves garlic, minced

Chopped cilantro, optional

Directions

1. In a large bowl, mix the meat, coconut milk, minced garlic, black pepper, grated ginger, lime juice, and sea salt. Cover with a lid and place in the refrigerator for at least 30 minutes. You can marinate it for up to 8 hours, if you wish.

2. Once the meat has marinated, place it in your Instant Pot along with the marinade, onions, carrots, tomatoes, and juice. Lock the lid and make sure the vent is in the Sealing position. Set the time for 20 minutes on the Manual setting.

3. Once the cooking is complete, let the pressure release naturally for 15 minutes before opening the lid.

4. Select the Sauté Normal mode and add in the diced zucchini. Simmer the ingredients for 5 to 6 minutes without covering the pot. The zucchini should be tender and the sauce should have thickened slightly.

5. Garnish with cilantro and serve. You can serve with rice or cauliflower rice, if you wish.

Potato Curry

Servings: 5

Ingredients

3 tablespoons of arrowroot powder or cornstarch

1 teaspoon of chili pepper flakes

Salt and pepper to taste

1 tablespoon of sugar, optional

2 heaping cups of chopped green beans

2 cups of water

2 tablespoons of curry powder

5 heaping cups of potatoes, no need to peel

4 large gloves of garlic, chopped finely

1 medium yellow onion, chopped

Directions

1. Press the Sauté function on your Instant Pot. Allow the Instant Pot to get hot before adding some drops of water. Proceed to cook the onions in the water until translucent. Add in garlic and let it cook for 1 more minute. Once done, press the Keep

Warm/Cancel function. If you don't have time, you can skip this first step and proceed to the second step.

2. Add the remaining ingredients except the arrowroot/cornstarch and the green beans into your Instant Pot. Select the Manual option and set the time for 20 minutes on High pressure. Once done, allow for natural pressure release.

3. Press the Keep Warm/Cancel function and then remove the lid carefully. Press the Sauté option. In a small bowl, combine a few tablespoons of water and the arrowroot/cornstarch. The mixture should be slurry. Pour the mixture inside your Instant Pot while stirring frequently.

4. Season with salt and pepper and then add green beans. Cook for 5 minutes. The green beans should be tender and the gravy should have thickened.

5. Remove and serve immediately.

Lentil Curry

Servings: 4 to 6

Ingredients

2 cups green or brown lentils

2 tablespoons of lemon juice

1 (14-ounce) can of light coconut milk

1/8 to ¼ teaspoon of cayenne pepper

¾ teaspoon of ground turmeric

1 teaspoon of kosher salt

½ tablespoon of coconut sugar or brown sugar

1 tablespoon plus 1 teaspoon curry powder

6 garlic cloves, minced

3 tablespoons minced fresh ginger

1 small shallot, finely chopped

½ tablespoon coconut oil

Chopped fresh cilantro, to garnish

Cooked brown rice, as staple

Directions

1. Rinse the lentils well and drain. Set aside. Select the Sauté function on your Instant Pot and then add the coconut oil. Allow the oil to melt and then add the shallot, 1 tablespoon of water, garlic, and ginger. Cook for 2 minutes or until very fragrant making sure you stir frequently. The shallot should be soft once done. Add the coconut sugar, curry powder, turmeric, cayenne, and salt and then stir vigorously. Don't breathe in the steam, as it is quite spicy.

2. Add the lentils, 1 cup of water, and the coconut milk. Stir well to make sure that lentils are completely coated with the liquid mixture. Hit the Cancel button to stop the Sauté function. Proceed to seal the lid and set the timer for 15 minutes on High pressure.

3. Once the cooking is complete, allow for natural pressure release and then vent. This will allow the pressure to release completely. Open the lid carefully and then stir in the lemon juice. You can adjust the seasoning, if you wish. You can also add some more water if you notice that the curry is too thick.

4. Sprinkle with cilantro and then serve with hot rice. Leftovers can be placed in the refrigerator for 4 to 5 days in an airtight container. You can also freeze for 2 to 3 months, if you wish.

Chicken Curry with Yogurt and Spinach

Servings: 6

Ingredients

1 teaspoon of garam masala

10 ounce of baby spinach

1.5 pounds of chicken thighs, boneless and skinless

½ cup of water

1 teaspoon of garam masala

2 teaspoons of turmeric

½ teaspoon of cayenne pepper

1 teaspoon of salt

2 tablespoons cornstarch

½ cup Greek yogurt

2 tomatoes, quartered

1 tablespoon minced ginger minced

1 tablespoon of garlic cloves minced

1 onion peeled and quartered

Directions

1. Put all the ingredients in a blender, except the spinach, chicken, and garam masala, and blend.

2. Layer the chicken in your Instant Pot and the chicken should be in large pieces. Pour the sauce over the chicken.

3. Press the Soup option and allow the food to cook for 8 minutes. Once done, allow for natural pressure release. This should take about 10 minutes.

4. Open the lid and then remove the chicken. Once done, press the Sauté function on your Instant Pot.

5. Roughly chop up the spinach and add it to the sauce. Slice the chicken into bite-size pieces and return them to your Instant Pot. Do not close the lid. Let the sauce simmer. This will allow it to thicken and the spinach to wilt.

6. Add in garam masala. This will add flavor to the dish.

7. Once done, serve with mashed potatoes, rice, naan, or cauliflower rice.

Instant Pot Mutton Curry

Servings: 2 to 4

Ingredients

1 ¼ cups (313ml) of unsalted chicken stock or water

½ cup (125 ml) of tomato paste

¼ teaspoon of mild Indian chili powder

3 tablespoons curry powder

2 tablespoons cooking oil

1 tablespoon cilantro, chopped

1 medium potato, quartered

1 tablespoon ginger, minced

1 medium shallot, minced

2 small onions, sliced or diced

8 garlic cloves, minced

Kosher salt and black pepper

1.1 lbs. (500g) of cubed frozen goat shoulder

Directions

1. Press the Sauté function on your Instant Pot and then adjust to Sauté. Once the Instant Pot indicator reads hot, add 1 tablespoon of cooking oil and then place the goat shoulder inside your Instant Pot. Season with black pepper and 2 pinches of salt. Brown for 5 minutes on all sides then remove. Set aside.

2. Press the Cancel function and then press the Sauté function. Add in 1 tablespoon of cooking oil, minced ginger, sliced onion, and shallot. Stir the ingredients for about 1 minute. Add the garlic. Cook for an additional 30 seconds as you stir frequently.

3. Add the curry powder and the Indian chili powder. Cook for 1 to 2 minutes stirring frequently. Add ¼ cup of chicken stock or water. Use a wooden spoon to deglaze the pot well. Add the remaining cup of chicken stock or water.

4. Return the goat shoulder plus all the meat juice inside your Instant Pot. Add ½ cup of tomato paste but do not stir the mixture. Arrange the quartered potatoes on top of the tomato paste and close the lid. Cook for 35 to 40 minutes in High pressure. Once

done, allow for full natural release. This should take about 15 minutes.

5. Carefully open the lid. Break up the cooked potatoes. This will allow the curry sauce to thicken. Add 1 tablespoon of chopped cilantro and stir. Adjust the seasoning, if needed. Remove and serve with naan or rice.

Simple Mutton Curry

Servings: 6

Ingredients

500 to 600 grams mutton (cut into medium sized pieces)

1 tablespoon of ghee, butter, or oil

1 tablespoon of kasuri methi

1 teaspoon of garam masala

2 potatoes, quartered

2 tablespoons of mutton masala

1 teaspoon of coriander powder

4 large tomatoes, finely chopped

1 tablespoon of ginger-garlic paste

3 large onions, finely chopped

1 green chili, sliced lengthwise

3 to 4 cloves

3 to 4 cardamom pods

1 (one-inch) cinnamon sticks

1 bay leaf

3 tablespoons of oil

Salt to taste

Directions

1. Turn on the Sauté function of your Instant Pot and add in oil. Then sauté the bay leaf, cloves, cinnamon, and cardamom for 1 minute. Add in the onions, green chili, and ginger-garlic paste. Next cook for 7 to 8 more minutes or until the onions are fragrant and translucent.

2. Add in tomatoes, mutton or meat masala, coriander powder, and then season with salt. Cook for 5 minutes to allow the tomatoes to break down slightly. Add in mutton, potatoes, and 1 cup of water. Close the lid properly. Cook for 45 minutes on High pressure. Once done, allow the pressure to release naturally.

3. Open the lid and press the Sauté function again. If the curry is too thick, you can add a little of water. Next, stir in the ghee, garam masala, and kasuri methi. Let the ingredients simmer for about 4 to 5 minutes. Once done, allow the curry to rest for about 15 minutes.

4. Serve and enjoy.

Gourd Curry

Servings: 3

Ingredients

2 teaspoons of salt

½ teaspoon of garam masala

¼ teaspoon of turmeric

2 teaspoons of coriander powder

1 tablespoon of lemon juice

2 tomatoes, chopped

1 onion, chopped

1 green chili pepper, optional

1 inch ginger, finely chopped

4 cloves of garlic, finely chopped

1 teaspoon of cumin seeds

1 tablespoon of oil

2 bottles gourd or lauki cut into about ½ inch pieces

Cilantro to garnish

Directions

1. Press the Sauté function and allow your Instant Pot to heat up. Sauté the garlic, green chilies, ginger, and cumin.

2. Once the garlic is golden brown, add the chopped onions. Cook for 2 minutes. Add the salt, chopped tomatoes, and spices. Make sure you scrape any ingredients sticking to the bottom of your Instant Pot. To do this, add 2 to 3 tablespoons of water and deglaze the pot.

3. Stir in the bottle gourd pieces and press Cancel. Close the lid and make sure that the vent is in the Sealing position.

4. Select 6 minutes on the Manual or pressure cook function. Once cooking is done, allow the pressure to release naturally. This should take 10 minutes.

5. Gently stir the curry and garnish it with some cilantro. Lauki curry can be served with rice or roti.

As you have noticed, most curries are served with roti, naan, and rice. In the following chapter, we will look at some rice recipes.

Chapter 4: Instant Pot Rice Recipes

Glossary Of Terms You Will Find In This Chapter

Basmati rice: A very long-grain Indian rice that has a delicate fragrance.

Biryani: Indian word that stands for a dish that is made up of highly seasoned rice with fish, seafood, meat, or vegetables.

Garam masala: A combination of ground spices.

Jeera: Indian word for cumin.

Pilaf: Rice that is cooked in a seasoned broth that consists of mixed spices and sometimes vegetables.

Raita: A mixture of onions, tomatoes, and yogurt.

Urad dal split: Split black gram lentils.

Indian Vegetable Rice

Servings: 4 to 6

Ingredients

1 ½ cups of brown long grain or basmati rice

1 cup of frozen peas

2 cups of low-sodium chicken broth

2 teaspoons of curry powder

1 teaspoon of coarse kosher salt

½ cup of chopped carrot, diced into small pieces

1 garlic clove, finely minced

¼ cup of chopped shallot

1 tablespoon of cooking oil

Directions

1. Press the Sauté function and once the pot is hot, heat the cooking oil. Then proceed to add the onion and sauté for 1 to 2 minutes or until translucent. Add garlic and rice. Stir well and cook for 30 more seconds.

2. Add in carrots, curry powder, chicken broth, and salt. Stir the mixture well to combine.

3. Close the lid properly and cook for 22 minutes on Manual High pressure.

4. Once the rice is done, allow for natural pressure release. If you don't have time, you can allow it to release naturally for 10 minutes before doing a quick release.

5. Open the lid and fluff the rice. Stir in the peas or toss to combine. You can adjust the seasoning; add more salt and pepper, if you wish.

6. Serve immediately.

Instant Pot Basmati Rice

Servings: 2 to 4

Ingredients

½ teaspoon salt, adjust to taste

1 cup water

1 tablespoon of oil of your choice

1 cup (250 ml) of long-grain basmati rice, soaked for 15 to 30 minutes

Directions

1. Place the basmati rice in a bowl and cover it with cold water. Allow it to soak for 15 to 30 minutes. Once done, drain, rinse well. Set aside.

2. Select the Sauté function and let the Instant Pot heat up for 1 minute. Add the oil and gently swirl it around to allow it to coat the bottom of the pot well. This will prevent the rice from sticking.

3. Add in rice and the water. Season the mixture with salt and stir to mix well.

4. Close the lid and make sure the pressure valve is closed. Select 6 minutes at High pressure.

5. Once the cooking time is up, do a natural pressure release. This will take 10 minutes. Once done, open the valve to allow any remaining pressure to release.

6. Use a fork to fluff the rice and then serve.

Chicken Biryani

Servings: 6 to 8

Ingredients

1 jalapeño, chopped into 8 rings, optional

6 boiled and shelled eggs, optional

1 teaspoon of saffron mixed in 1 tablespoon of warm milk

2 teaspoons of salt

2 bay leaves

2 large onions, thinly sliced

3 tablespoons of ghee, divided

3 cups of Basmati rice

Marinade:

2 lb. whole bone-in skinless chicken cut into 12 pieces

2 teaspoons salt

¾ cup plain yogurt

2 tablespoons lemon juice

¼ cup of chopped cilantro

¼ cup of mint leaves

½ teaspoon of turmeric

1 tablespoon of red chili powder

1 tablespoon of garlic cloves, minced

1 tablespoon of ginger grated

2 teaspoons of garam masala

Directions

1. Prepare the marinade by combining the garam masala, garlic paste, turmeric, ginger paste, red chili powder, yogurt, mint leaves, half the chopped cilantro, lemon juice, and salt. Use the marinade to coat the chicken evenly before placing it in the refrigerator for 30 minutes.

2. In the meantime, wash the basmati rice. Soak it in water for 20 minutes.

3. Press the Sauté function on your Instant Pot. Allow the pot to become hot. Add 2 tablespoons of ghee. Add the onions and cook for 15 minutes, as you stir frequently. Once done, remove half the onions. Set aside. You'll use the reserved onion to garnish the biryani.

4. Add 1 more tablespoon of ghee and bay leaves to the pot. You can add sliced jalapeño, if you wish, for your biryani to be extra spicy. Add in the marinated chicken and proceed to mix well. You can use a spatula to deglaze the pot.

5. If you're cooking chicken on bone, close the lid and make sure the pressure valve is set to Sealing and then select 4 minutes on Manual mode. Once done, do a quick release and stir the chicken. If you are cooking chicken breasts, mix well and cook for 3 minutes on Sauté mode.

6. Carefully drain the rice and proceed to pour it over the chicken. Season with 2 teaspoons of salt and add 3 cups of water. Close your Instant Pot, turn the valve to Sealing and select 6 minutes on Manual mode. Once done, do a quick release.

7. Fluff the rice and garnish with the reserved caramelized onions, cilantro, and saffron.

8. Serve with hard-boiled egg, Raita (a mixture of onions, tomatoes, and yogurt), and lemon wedges.

Instant Pot Lemon Rice

Servings: 3 to 4

Ingredients

Juice of ½ lemon, add after cooking

1 cup + 2 tablespoons water

¼ cup fried onions, optional

½ teaspoon ground cumin

½ teaspoon turmeric powder

½ teaspoon salt

1 cup (250 ml) of long-grain basmati rice, rinsed 2 to 3 times

3 to 4 whole green chilies, tops off

1 teaspoon urad dal split (split black gram lentils), rinsed and dried

1 teaspoon of brown mustard seeds

1 teaspoon of ghee, butter, or cooking oil

Directions

1. Rinse the basmati rice well until the water is clear. Drain. Set aside. Rinse the split lentils and drain. Set aside.

2. Press the Sauté High mode on your Instant Pot and allow the pot to become hot. Add the split black gram lentils and the mustard seeds.

3. Once the mustard seeds begin to splutter, add the green chilies, spices, and the rice. You can add some fried onions, if you wish. Cook for 1 to 2 minutes. Add the water and close the lid properly. Set the time for 6 minutes on the Manual setting. Make sure the vent is at the Sealing position.

4. Once done, allow for 5 minutes of natural pressure release and then manually release the remaining pressure.

5. Open the lid and use a fork to fluff the rice. Drizzle some lemon juice on top and mix well.

6. Enjoy.

Vegetable Pilaf

Servings: 4

Ingredients

Whole spices

4 cloves

1 star anise

1 stick cinnamon

1 teaspoon of cumin seeds

1 bay leaf

Spices

1 teaspoon of salt

½ teaspoon garam masala

½ teaspoon of cayenne or red chili powder

½ teaspoon of turmeric

Other ingredients

1 ¼ cups of water

2 cups of mixed vegetables (carrots, green beans, peas, corn, edamame)

1 medium potato, cut into small pieces

½ cup of tomatoes, chopped

½ tablespoon of garlic cloves, minced

½ tablespoon of minced ginger

½ cup of onion, sliced

1 green chili pepper, optional

1 tablespoon of ghee, butter, or oil

1 cup (250 ml) of long-grain basmati rice, rinsed

Directions

1. Press the Sauté function on your Instant Pot and allow the pot to heat. Add in ghee and whole spices and then proceed to cook them for 30 seconds. The cumin seeds should change color.

2. Once the spices start to splutter, add the onion, ginger, garlic, and green chili. Then cook for 2 minutes or until the onion is translucent. Add the tomatoes and spices. Stir the mixture to mix well.

3. Add the potato and the mixed vegetables. Stir to mix.

4. Add rice and water to combine with the vegetables. Deglaze the pot to remove

anything stuck on it. Close the lid properly and make sure the vent is in the Sealing position.

5. Select 4 minutes at High pressure on the Manual setting.

6. Once the cooking is done, let the pressure release naturally. This should take 10 minutes. Once done, release the pressure manually.

7. Gently fluff the vegetable pilaf. You can serve with raita or homemade yogurt, if you wish.

Instant Pot Rice with Cumin Seeds

Servings: 2

Ingredients

1 ½ cups of water

1 tablespoon of fresh coriander

Salt to taste

1 bay leaf

1 inch piece cinnamon

2 to 3 cloves

1 to 2 green cardamom

2 slit green chili

2 teaspoons of cumin seeds

2 tablespoons of ghee, butter, or oil

1 cup (250 ml) of long-grain basmati rice

Directions

1. Select the Sauté mode on your Instant Pot and wait for the pot to become hot. Add oil or ghee once the pot is hot then add in cinnamon sticks, bay leaf, cumin seeds (also

known as jeera), and cardamom. Next, cook for 30 seconds or until fragrant.

2. Add the green chilies. Cook for 30 more seconds.

3. Add in basmati rice, salt, and water. Stir the mixture to combine.

4. Press Cancel on your Instant Pot and close the lid. Make sure you turn the valve from the Venting to the Setting position.

5. Set the time for 5 minutes at High pressure on Manual function.

6. Once the rice is done, do a quick release. Be careful not to get burnt by the hot steam.

7. Carefully remove the lid. Garnish with coriander leaves or fresh cilantro.

8. Serve and enjoy.

Beetroot Rice

Servings: 2

Ingredients

1 tablespoon of lemon juice

2 cups of water

Salt as needed

2 tablespoons of chopped coriander leaves

A few curry leaves, optional

A handful of mint leaves, optional

1 teaspoon of coriander powder

1 teaspoon of biryani masala or garam masala

1 teaspoon of cumin seeds

1 tablespoon of ginger-garlic paste

3 slit green chili

½ cup green peas (you can use frozen)

1 cup grated beetroot

1 medium onion thinly sliced

1 cup (250 ml) of long-grain basmati rice

For the seasoning:

1 cardamom

1 inch piece of cinnamon

2 cloves

1 bay leaf

2 tablespoons oil

Directions

1. Select the Sauté function on the Instant Pot. Once the pot is hot, heat the oil, and then add in bay leaf, curry leaves, cinnamon sticks, cumin, cloves, and cardamom. Sauté for 30 seconds or until fragrant.

2. Add the ginger-garlic paste and the green chilies. Cook for 1 to 2 minutes.

3. Add the sliced onions and cook for 1 to 2 minutes.

4. Add the sliced onions and cook for 2 to 3 more minutes or until the onions turn translucent. Make sure you stir the ingredients frequently.

5. Add the grated beetroot and the green peas. Sauté for 2 more minutes.

6. Add the coriander powder and the biryani powder. Stir to combine.

7. Add water, salt, and rinsed basmati rice. Stir once more.

8. Press Cancel on your Instant Pot and close the lid properly. The valve should be at the Sealing position.

9. Select the Manual/Pressure cook option and set the time for 6 minutes on High pressure.

10. Once the time is up, wait for the pressure to release naturally. This should take 10 minutes. You need to be careful due to the hot steam.

11. Remove the lid. Garnish the beetroot rice with lime juice and cilantro.

12. Serve and enjoy.

Instant Pot Shrimp Curry and Rice

Servings: 2

Ingredients

For cooking Basmati Rice:

1 teaspoon of ghee, butter, or oil

1¼ cups of water

1/8 teaspoon of turmeric powder

¼ teaspoon of garam masala

½ teaspoon of salt

¾ cup of mixed veggies, cut very small

1 cup (250 ml) of long-grain basmati rice, rinsed

For making Shrimp Curry:

¾ cup of water

2 handfuls of cilantro, chopped

¼ teaspoon of salt

2 teaspoons coriander powder

¼ teaspoon of garam masala

1/8 teaspoon of turmeric powder

¾ to 1 teaspoon (based on your spice level) chili powder

2 tomatoes, chopped

1 teaspoon garlic ginger paste

1 teaspoon of salt

2 onions, chopped

¾ teaspoon of cumin seeds

2 dried bay leaves

1 tablespoon of oil

For marinating shrimp:

½ teaspoon of salt

¼ teaspoon of garam masala

1/8 teaspoon of turmeric powder

½ teaspoon of chili powder

15 to 20 shrimp, deveined

Directions

1. In a bowl, add the marinade ingredients and marinate the shrimp for 5 minutes.

2. Turn on your Instant Pot and select the Sauté option.

3. Once the display changes to HOT, add the oil. Once the oil is hot, add the cumin seeds and dried bay leaves. Cook for several seconds.

4. Add the onion and ¼ teaspoon salt and cook for 1 minute.

5. Add the ginger-garlic paste and cook for 2 more minutes. Add the tomatoes and cook for an additional 1 minute.

6. Add the marinated shrimp, garam masala, chili powder, coriander powder, turmeric powder, and salt. Stir to combine well.

7. Add the water and cilantro. Stir again.

8. Carefully place the trivet over the shrimp in your Instant Pot.

9. Place the rice ingredients in a glass or stainless steel bowl. The bowl should be heat resistant.

10. Place the bowl carefully on the trivet and close the lid. Make sure you turn the vent to the Sealing position.

11. Cancel the Sauté mode and select 7 minutes on Manual High pressure.

12. Once cooking is complete, allow for natural pressure release. This should take 10 minutes. Once done, proceed to do a quick release.

13. Open the lid, take out the rice bowl. Remove the trivet.

14. Click the Sauté mode and cook the shrimp for 5 minutes. This will allow the shrimp curry to thicken.

15. Serve the rice and shrimp curry.

Instant Pot Fried Rice

Servings: 4

Ingredients

2 cups long grain rice

2 medium eggs

½ cup of frozen peas

3 tablespoons cooking oil

2 carrots

2½ cups vegetable broth

Salt and pepper to taste

Directions

1. Add the vegetable stock and the rice into your Instant Pot, and mix well. The rice should be evenly spread. Add diced carrots and close the lid. Turn the vent to the Sealing position and select 3 minutes on the Manual setting.

2. Once the cooking is complete, press the Cancel button and allow the pressure to release naturally. This will take 10 minutes. Afterwards, release the pressure manually.

3. Fluff the rice. It will be a bit sticky. Move the rice to the side of your Instant Pot and select the Sauté function. Add oil to the other side and the frozen peas and cook for 1 minute. Once time is up, mix all the ingredients together.

4. Proceed to make a well or hole in the middle of the rice. Carefully add the beaten eggs into the well and stir the eggs into the rice. Fry for 1 to 2 minutes and then turn off your Instant Pot. Adjust the seasoning if needed.

5. Serve and enjoy.

Instant Pot Vegetable Rice

Servings: 6

Ingredients

3 cups basmati rice

5 to 8 tablespoons of cashew paste

1 tablespoon of organic tomato paste (or use 1 tomato)

½ teaspoon of cinnamon powder

½ teaspoon of black pepper powder

2 cloves, powdered

½ teaspoon of red chili powder

1 teaspoon of cumin powder

1 ½ tablespoons of ground coriander

Salt to taste

½ inch ginger

1 garlic clove

1 cup of chopped red onion

2 large carrots

1 cup of green beans

3 ½ cups water

Directions

1. Add the oil into your Instant Pot and press the Sauté mode. Allow the oil to heat and then add in ginger and garlic. Cook for 1 minute as you stir constantly.

2. Add the onions and sauté for 1 minute.

3. Add the spices, stir frequently, and add tomato paste, green beans, and carrots. Stir well. Cook for 1 to 2 minutes.

4. Add the cashew paste. Stir to combine.

5. Add in the water and the rice and then stir to combine well. You should aim for an even mix.

6. Close the lid well and turn the vent to the Sealing position. Select the Pressure Cook setting and set time for 4 minutes. Once the cooking time is up, let the pressure release naturally. This should take 10 minutes.

7. Once the time is up, open the lid and carefully remove the pot.

8. Serve with a side dish, if you wish.

After curries and rice, the next thing that comes to mind when you mention Indian cuisine is lentils. Learn some lentil recipes that you can prepare in your Instant Pot, in the next chapter.

Chapter 5: Instant Pot Lentil and Legume Recipes

Glossary Of Terms You Will Find In This Chapter

Chana: Hindi name for chickpea or garbanzo beans.

Masala: A mixture of various spices.

Pav: An Indian word for bread.

Ladipav: Dinner rolls or buns.

Kasuri methi. A semi-arid crop that is cultivated worldwide. Its leaves consist of three tiny obviate to almost oblong leaflets. Indians usually use its seeds in their ingredients and that is exactly what you should use in this recipe.

Masoor dal. Red lentil.

Dal: Split pulses of lentils.

Sambar: A dish that consists of vegetables and lentils cooked with tamarind and other spies.

Toor dal: Pigeon pea.

Serrano: Capsicum annum, which is a type of chili pepper that comes from Mexico.

Rajma: A vegetarian dish that is made of red kidney beans combined with thick gravy that has whole spices.

Trivet: A three legged metal stand that is placed over a fire for a kettle or a cooking pot on which to stand.

Pongal: An Indian dish that consists of rice that is cooked with various herbs and spices.

Urad dal: A white lentil with a black skin.

Asafoetida: A brownish gum that comes from various plants. It has a strong taste and odor.

Jiggery: Raw sugar that Indians use to flavor their dishes which include vegetable curries. Indians also consume jiggery as is.

Moong dal: Skinned and split mung beans.

Papad: A thin crisp wafer that is made from chickpea flour or lentil that is cooked with dry heat or fried.

Kara boondi: An Indian dessert that is made from sweetened fried chickpea.

Bisi bele bath: A spicy lentil- and rice-based dish.

Hing: The English word for hing is asafoetida (also spelled without an "o" as asafetida). It is a sticky liquid that has a strong smell. It comes from the roots of plants.

Haldi: Indian word for turmeric.

Dal tadka: Tempering of lentils.

Jeera: Indian word for cumin.

Kadi patta: Curry leaves.

Mirchi: Chili powder or chili pepper.

Kashmiri: A spice that is relatively mild in heat and full of flavor. It is similar to paprika.

Rai: Mustard seed.

Paratha: Flatbread.

Amchoor: A mango powder that Indians use to add a sour, tangy, and fruity flavor.

Chipotle: Smoke dried jalapeño.

Pappu Charu: Pappu means dal, which stands for lentils. Charu means rasam, which stands for a thin flavored consistency pulp that is cooked with dal.

Sultani dal: A lentil dish that is cooked with rich ingredients.

Curry Spinach Chickpea Masala

Servings: 6 to 8

Ingredients

1 tablespoon of roasted chickpea flour

2 cups of fresh tomato purée

1 ½ cups of water

½ tablespoon of grated ginger

1 tablespoon of grated garlic

1 bay leaf

1 cup of chopped onions

3 tablespoons of cooking oil

1 cup raw chickpeas, to be soaked

Spices

1 teaspoon of coriander powder

1 tablespoon of cholay or chana masala

2 teaspoons of cayenne pepper powder or red mirch powder

½ teaspoon of turmeric

1 green chili finely chopped

To be added later:

Lemon

A handful of chopped fresh cilantro

Salt to taste

2 cups chopped baby spinach

Directions

1. The night before, wash the chickpeas in cold running water for about 30 seconds and put them in a pot with 2 cups of water. Bring the chickpeas to a boil and allow it to boil for 5 minutes. Once done, allow it to soak overnight or for 8 to 10 hours.

2. Drain the excess water.

3. Press the Sauté function and allow the pot to become hot. Add the 3 tablespoons of cooking oil.

4. Add the onions and sauté for 2 minutes or until the onions are translucent.

5. Add the garlic paste, ginger, bay leaf, and green chili. Sauté for 20 seconds.

6. Add the chili powder, chana masala, coriander powder, turmeric, and 1

tablespoon of water and stir to mix them all. Cook for 10 seconds.

7. Add the roasted chickpea flour (besan). Cook for 10 more seconds.

8. Add the drained chickpeas, tomato purée and 1 ½ cups of water. Stir to combine well.

9. Close the lid properly and set the time for 15 minutes on Manual High   pressure. The steam release should be at the Sealing position.

10. Once the timer goes off, allow for 15 minutes natural pressure release.

11. Open the lid and stir well. The chickpeas should be easy to mash. Press the Sauté mode and season with salt. Add the chopped spinach and use a spoon to mash some chickpeas. Cook for 3 minutes and then switch off the Instant Pot.

12. Garnish with lemon juice and chopped coriander and serve as a soup. You can serve with quinoa, rice, or roti.

Instant Pot Dal Fry

Servings: 2

Ingredients

2 tablespoons cilantro or coriander leaves, chopped finely

1 teaspoon of lemon juice

½ teaspoon of kasuri methi (dried fenugreek leaves)

½ teaspoon of garam masala

2 ¼ cups of water

Salt

1 teaspoon of coriander powder

1 teaspoon of red chili powder

½ teaspoon of turmeric powder

½ cup of tomato

1 teaspoon of garlic paste or freshly grated

1 teaspoon of ginger paste, freshly grated or crushed

1 green chili

½ cup of onion

2 tablespoons of oil

2 tablespoons of masoor dal

2 tablespoons of yellow moong dal (split and skinless)

¼ cup arhar dal (toor dal or split pigeon peas)

Directions

1. Wash the dals and then soak them in water for 15 to 30 minutes. You can skip the soaking part if you don't have time.

2. Select the Sauté mode on your Instant Pot. Wait until the display says hot and then add the oil. Once the oil is hot, add the cumin seeds and let them sizzle.

3. Add the onions and cook them for 1 to 2 minutes.

4. Mix the green chili and ginger-garlic paste. Add the mixture into your Instant Pot and cook for 40 to 50 seconds. The raw smell should go away.

5. Add the tomatoes and sauté for 2 minutes; the tomatoes should be soft.

6. Add the coriander powder, turmeric powder, chili powder, and salt; stir to mix together.

7. Add the dal and the water and stir to mix.

8. Cover your Instant Pot and make sure the vent is in the Sealing position. If you have soaked the dal first, set the time for 5 minutes on the Manual setting. If you did not soak the dal, set the time for 7 minutes on the Manual setting.

9. Once cooking is done, allow for 5 minutes natural release followed by quick release. If the dal fry needs more water, add a bit of water and cook for several minutes on the Sauté mode.

10. Add the kasuri methi, lemon juice, and garam masala and stir well to combine.

11. Garnish with coriander leaves and serve.

Instant Pot Eggplant Sambar

Servings: 4

Ingredients

1 tablespoon of tamarind pulp

2 ½ to 4 cups of water, more for saucepan

1 cup split pigeon peas, washed and soaked for 15 minutes and drained

1 teaspoon salt

½ cup chopped green bell pepper or ½ cup chopped carrots

1 or 2 cups of chopped eggplant (you can also use other veggies)

½ teaspoon ground turmeric

1 2/ cups or 2 medium tomatoes, chopped

1 tablespoon of sambar powder or use 2 teaspoons coriander powder + a good pinch of cumin, cayenne, and black pepper

½ cup chopped red onion or sliced pearl onions

3 cloves garlic, chopped

10 curry leaves, coarsely chopped

2 dried red chilies, optional

¼ teaspoon fenugreek seeds, optional

½ teaspoon black mustard seeds

1 teaspoon of safflower or other neutral oil

Cilantro and lemon for garnish

Directions

1. Press the Sauté button and once the pot is hot, heat the oil. Add the mustard seeds and sauté for 10 seconds or until they pop. Add the red chilies, fenugreek seeds, and curry leaves. Cook for several seconds before adding the onion and garlic. Cook for 5 minutes or until the onion turns translucent.

2. Add the sambar powder into the Instant Pot. Cook for 30 more seconds. Add the tomatoes and the turmeric and stir to mix. Cook for 6 to 8 minutes or until the tomatoes become saucy. Pour in the vegetables. Mix well.

3. Add the tamarind, drained split peas, water, and salt. Mix well and close the lid. Cook for 10 to 15 minutes. Once done, allow the pressure to release naturally. You can add

more tamarind extract, if you wish. Add more salt if needed. You can also add a pinch of sugar, if you need to balance the tang.

4. Garnish with lemon juice and cilantro. Serve over rice or steamed rice cakes or use it as a soup.

Vegetable Sambar

Servings: 2 to 4

Ingredients

Tempering Ingredients:

1 sprig or 10 to 15 curry leaves

1 tablespoon of cumin seeds

1 tablespoon of mustard seeds

7 to 8 garlic, crushed and chopped

3 tablespoons of ghee (vegans can substitute with oil of choice)

Spices:

2 tablespoons of sambar powder

1 tablespoon of turmeric

1 tablespoon of coriander powder

1 tablespoon of red chili powder

Other ingredients:

Water as needed

½ cup cilantro

1 small lime-sized tamarind or 1 tablespoon concentrate

1 cup of pigeon peas/toor dal

1 big diced tomato

1 small diced bottle gourd

1 carrot, diced

Salt to taste

1 Serrano pepper, quartered

½ onion, cubed

1 tablespoon of oil

Directions

1. Select the Sauté High mode and then heat the oil. Sauté the onions and the Serrano pepper.

2. Add your favorite veggies and fry for 1 minute. Add the spices and stir to mix.

3. Add the lentils, tamarind, water, and salt.

4. Turn off the Sauté mode and then select 12 minutes on Manual high.

5. Once cooked, allow for natural pressure release. Proceed to extract the tamarind

juice from the pulp. Add it to your Instant Pot. Adjust the salt and spices if need be and then boil for several minutes. Turn off the pot.

6. Do the tempering and then add it to the ingredients in the Instant Pot. Add cilantro and serve while hot. You can serve with rice and potato chips, if you wish.

Instant Pot Kidney Beans

Servings: 6

Ingredients

For the Kidney Beans

2 cups water (to cook the beans)

1 cup dried red kidney beans, soaked in hot water for an hour

For the Onion Masala

1/3 cup of water

1 teaspoon of ground coriander

1 teaspoon of salt

1 teaspoon of ground cumin seeds

1 teaspoon of garam masala

1 teaspoon of turmeric

1 teaspoon of cayenne pepper

1 cup of diced canned tomatoes with liquid

1 tablespoon of garlic cloves, minced

1 tablespoon minced ginger

1 ½ cups of onion diced

1 tablespoon of oil

Directions

1. Place the onion masala ingredients in your Instant Pot and then carefully place the trivet on top.

2. Place 2 cups of water and the red kidney beans in a bowl. Make sure that the bowl is heat-safe. Cover the bowl well, using some foil. This will prevent the contents from spilling into the other ingredients.

3. Place the bowl on top of the trivet in the Instant Pot. Close the lid and make sure the valve is in the Sealing position.

4. Select the Bean option. This will cook the beans for 30 minutes. Once cooking is complete, allow for natural pressure release. This will take 10 minutes

5. Once done, open your Instant Pot and carefully remove the beans. Remove the trivet and then proceed to slightly mash at least half of the red kidney beans (rajma). You can use the back of a spoon to mash the beans.

6. Select the Sauté High function on the Instant Pot. Add the red kidney beans

(rajma) and whatever water remained in the pot. Mix it well with the onion masala. Allow the contents in the pot to come to a boil to make sure all the flavors mix well.

7. Remove and serve with rice.

Tiffin Sambar

Servings: 2 to 4

Ingredients

To temper:

¼ teaspoon turmeric powder

½ teaspoon urad dal

1 sprig curry leaves

2 pinches asafoetida (also known as hing)

¼ teaspoon cumin seeds

½ teaspoon mustard seeds

1 tablespoon of oil

For the masala paste:

Salt as needed

2 tablespoons of grated coconut

2 tablespoons of fried gram dal (pottukadalai)

1 heaped tablespoon sambar powder

1 large tomato

1 onion chopped

1 tablespoon or less jiggery (depending on the sourness of your tamarind)

1 tablespoon of thick tamarind pulp

Other ingredients:

A handful of coriander leaves

7 to 8 pearl onions, peeled

1 large tomato, chopped

1 cup chopped veggies (carrots / pumpkin)

¼ cup moong dal (soaked for 30 minutes)

Directions

1. First soak the dal for 30 or more minutes. You can soak the dal overnight, if you wish. If you're pressed for time, you can allow the dal to soak as you prepare the other ingredients.

2. Grind the ingredients for the masala paste. If you'll be using tamarind, you can grind them after heating. This will make the tamarind easier to grind.

3. Press the Sauté mode and then heat the oil. Once it's hot, add the tempering ingredients and allow the mustard seeds to splutter.

4. Add the onions and cook for 1 minute. Add the tomatoes and proceed to cook for 1 more minute and then add the chopped vegetables. Switch the Sauté mode off.

5. Add the soaked dal, ground mixture, and 2 ½ cups of water into your Instant Pot. Close the lid properly and select 10 minutes on Manual High pressure. Once done, you should do a natural pressure release.

6. Open the lid and mix everything well. You can adjust the consistency by adding more water, if needed. Add fresh coriander leaves. Serve hot with pongal.

Lentil Rice

Servings: 4

For Tempering (This is optional):

2 dry chilies

Cashew nuts

1 tablespoon of ghee (can use oil also)

Other ingredients

Salt

½ teaspoon, turmeric powder/haldi

A pinch asafoetida/hing

1 sprig curry leaves

½ teaspoon cumin (jeera) seeds

1 teaspoon mustard seeds

2 to 3 tablespoons oil

2 tablespoons cilantro (coriander) leaves

½ teaspoon jiggery

3 tablespoons of bisi bele bath (hot lentil rice dish) powder

6 cups water

1 medium sized onion

2 tablespoons tamarind extract (2 tablespoons of tamarind water extracted from soaking small lemon size tamarind)

2 ½ cups mixed vegetables (bell pepper/capsicum, carrot, peas, beans, potato)

¾ cup toor dal/spilt pigeon peas

1 cup rice

Directions

1. Chop the vegetables and the onions. Set aside.

2. In a bowl, soak the tamarind in warm water. Next, extract the pulp. Set aside.

3. Select the Sauté mode and once the pot is hot, heat the oil. Once the oil is hot, add the cumin, curry leaves, and mustard seeds. Allow the ingredients to splutter.

4. Add the onions and cook for 2 to 3 minutes or until they turn translucent. Make sure you stir the mixture frequently.

5. Add the mixed vegetables and sauté for 1 to 2 more minutes.

6. Add the turmeric powder, bisi bele bath powder, tamarind extract, and salt. Stir frequently to prevent the mixture from burning.

7. Add the lentils (toor dal), jiggery, rice, and water. Stir to combine.

8. Press Cancel and then close the lid. Make sure the valve is set to Sealing. Select 8 minutes on the Manual/pressure cook setting.

9. Once you hear the beep, do a natural pressure release.

10. Remove the lid carefully and then garnish with cilantro. Mix well.

11. Press the Sauté function and then add ½ to 1 cup of water. Boil the ingredients for 2 to 3 minutes. Once the bisi bele bath is ready, you can add tempering again, if you wish.

12. Serve with potato chips, kara boondi, and papad, if you wish.

Dal Tadka (Lentils with Spices and Herbs)

Servings: 4

Ingredients

For Basmati Rice:

1 teaspoon of salt, optional

1 tablespoon of ghee, butter, or oil, optional

1 ¼ cups of water

1 cup (250 ml) of long-grain basmati rice

Spices:

1 teaspoon of salt

½ teaspoon of red chili or mirchi powder

½ teaspoon of coriander (dhaniya) powder

¼ teaspoon turmeric

Other ingredients

3 cups water

1 cup split pigeon pea, washed

1 tomato, finely chopped

½ onion, finely chopped

3 cloves garlic

¼ teaspoon asafetida/hing

6 curry leaves (kadi patta)

1 teaspoon of cumin seeds (jeera)

1 tablespoon of ghee, butter, or oil

Cilantro to garnish

Directions

1. Press the Sauté function and then heat the oil. Add the garlic, green chili, cumin seeds, asafetida, and curry leaves.

2. Once the garlic is light brown, add the onions, and cook for 2 minutes. The onions should turn golden brown.

3. Add tomato and spices. Cook for 2 more minutes.

4. Add the dal and the water. Stir the ingredients well.

5. Carefully place the trivet inside your Instant Pot. Pour in the ingredients for the basmati rice in a bowl, and then place the bowl on the trivet. Make sure the bowl is heatproof. Close the lid properly and check to make

sure that the valve is in the Sealing position. Select 5 minutes on Manual High pressure.

6. Once you hear the beep, allow for natural pressure release. This should take 5 minutes. Once time is up, release the pressure manually for another 5 minutes.

7. Use tongs to carefully remove the bowl containing the basmati rice and then proceed to remove the trivet.

8. Garnish this dal tadka dish with cilantro and stir to mix. You can garnish it with lemon juice from half a lemon, if you wish.

Serve and enjoy.

Mango Dal

Servings: 4

Ingredients

3 cups water

½ teaspoon cayenne, optional

¼ teaspoon turmeric

1 teaspoon of salt

1 tomato chopped

½ onion chopped

2 red chili whole Kashmiri, optional

5 curry leaves (kadi patta)

½ teaspoon rai (mustard seeds)

1 tablespoon of ghee, butter, or oil

1 ripe mango, skin removed and cut into small pieces

1 cup split pigeon pea, washed

Cilantro to garnish

Directions

1. Press the Sauté function and heat the oil. Add the red chili, mustard seeds, and the curry leaves.

2. Once the mustard seeds start spluttering, add the chopped onion and let cook for 2 minutes.

3. Add the tomatoes, cayenne, turmeric powder, and salt.

4. Add the water and the lentils and stir well to mix. Press "Cancel" and then close the lid properly. Make sure the vent is in the Sealing position.

5. Select the Manual or Pressure Cook setting and set the time for 3 minutes. Once the cooking is done, do a quick release.

6. Carefully open the lid and proceed to add the mango pieces. Simmer the ingredients for 2 minutes or until the dal boils.

7. Remove and garnish with cilantro before serving.

Kale and Chick Peas

Servings: 2 to 4

Ingredients

1/8 cup water

1 teaspoon of dry mango or amchoor powder

½ teaspoon rai or mustard seeds

2 red chili peppers sliced, or green chili pepper

5 garlic cloves

½ large onion, sliced

1 tablespoon of oil

½ lb. baby kale leaves or kale leaves, chopped

½ cup chana dal (split chickpeas), washed (125 ml)

Spices:

¼ teaspoon turmeric (haldi) powder

½ teaspoon cayenne or red chili powder

½ teaspoon salt

2 teaspoons coriander (dhaniya) powder

Directions

1. Soak the chana dal in water for at least 1 hour. Once the time is up, drain the water. Set aside.

2. Select the Sauté mode of your Instant Pot and heat the oil. Add the garlic, red chili, and mustard seeds.

3. Once the garlic is golden brown, add the chopped onions. Sauté for 4 minutes as you stir frequently.

4. Add the spices and the chana dal. Stir to mix well and then cook for 2 minutes.

5. Add the kale leaves and 1/8 cup of water. Mix well.

6. Cancel the Sauté mode and set the time for 3 minutes on the Manual setting. Make sure the vent is in the Sealing position.

7. Once cooking time is up, do a quick release and then add the dry mango powder. If you need to add more water, add it and cook for a few more minutes on the Sauté function. Stir the kale chana dal frequently.

8. Remove and serve with paratha or roti.

Kidney Bean Chili

Servings: 2

Ingredients

½ cup fresh or frozen corn

¾ teaspoon salt

2 cups water, less or more depending on consistency preferred, use 1 ½ cups, if using cooked lentils

¼ cup celery, chopped

½ red bell pepper, chopped

2 to 3 teaspoons taco spice blend (the recipe is below)

½ teaspoon chipotle pepper powder

2 medium tomatoes, chopped

2 cloves of garlic, chopped

1 green chili, chopped

½ red onion chopped

2 teaspoons oil

1 cup kidney beans, cooked or canned

½ cup dry lentils or 1 cup cooked brown lentils

Pickled jalapeño, tortilla strips, lemon juice, cilantro, guacamole, yogurt/sour cream, for garnish

Directions

1. Use hot water to soak the lentils in a bowl for 30 minutes. Drain. Set aside.

2. Press the Sauté function and once it says hot, add the oil. Once the oil is hot, add the onion. Sauté for 4 minutes or until translucent.

3. Add the garlic and green chili pepper. Sauté for 2 more minutes.

4. Add the tomatoes, taco spice, and chipotle pepper. Cook for 5 minutes. The tomatoes should turn saucy.

5. Add the celery and the bell pepper. Stir to mix. Cook for 1 minute.

6. Add the kidney beans, drained lentils, 1 cup of water, salt and mix well. Close the lid and select 7 to 9 minutes on Manual High pressure. Once the cooking is complete, allow the pressure to release naturally.

7. Taste and adjust the seasoning accordingly. Garnish and serve.

Sweet Potato Lentil Curry

Servings: 4

Ingredients

2 cups water

3 cups water for the saucepan

¾ teaspoon salt

1 cup cubed sweet potatoes

1 cup (heaping) chopped eggplant

15 ounce can of tomatoes or 2 tomatoes, chopped

½ teaspoon ground coriander or ground cumin

½ to 1 teaspoon garam masala

¼ teaspoon turmeric

½ or 1 hot green chili, chopped

An inch of ginger, chopped

4 cloves of garlic, chopped

½ onion, chopped

1 teaspoon of oil, or use water to sauté to make oil-free

¾ cup lentils, soaked in warm hot water for at least 15 minutes

Pepper flakes for garnish

Cayenne and lemon to taste

A big handful of spinach

Directions

1. Soak the lentils in a bowl, as you prepare the other ingredients. Press the Sauté mode on your Instant Pot and then add the oil. Once the oil is hot, add the onion, ginger, garlic, and a pinch of salt. Sauté for 2 to 3 minutes ensuring that you stir the ingredients frequently.

2. Add the spices and stir to mix them in. Add the tomatoes and sauté for 4 to 5 minutes. You should mash the larger pieces.

3. Add the veggies, lentils, water, and salt. Stir to combine well.

4. Close the lid well. The valve should be in the Sealing position. Select 11 to 12 minutes on Manual High pressure. Once done, allow for natural pressure release.

5. Open the lid and add the spinach, lemon, and cayenne. Let the ingredients sit for 2

minutes. Alternatively, you can sauté for 2 minutes. You can add more water or a bit of nondairy milk, if you wish, to have a creamier consistency. Mix well. Taste the seasoning, then add more spices and salt, if needed.

6. Serve the curry with rice or flat bread. You can also serve it with crackers, if you wish.

Tangy Lentils (Pappu Charu)

Servings: 2

Ingredients

Main Ingredients:

3 cups water or as needed

1 cup dal or yellow pigeon peas

Cilantro to garnish

Salt to taste

Red chili powder to taste

1 teaspoon of coriander powder

1 inch Tamarind (extract the juice by soaking in hot water)

2 small tomatoes, chopped

½ onion roughly chopped

2 slit green chili

Tempering:

1 sprig curry leaves

3 to 4 cloves of garlic, crushed

1 broken red chili

½ heaping teaspoon turmeric powder

½ teaspoon cumin seeds

½ teaspoon mustard seeds

2 tablespoons ghee, butter, or oil

Directions

1. Select the Sauté High mode on your Instant Pot.

2. Add the oil and allow it to get hot. Add the tempering ingredients. You should add them one by one. Sauté for 1 to 2 minutes.

3. Add the onion and the green chili. Cook for 2 minutes.

4. Add the tomatoes and sauté for 2 more minutes.

5. Add the coriander powder, tamarind extract, red chili powder, water, dal, and salt. Mix well.

6. Turn off the Sauté function and then close the lid. Make sure the vent is in the Sealing position.

7. Once cooking is complete, proceed to do natural pressure release. This will take 10 minutes. Alternatively, you can do a quick

release, after leaving it in the warm mode for 10 minutes.

8. Garnish with cilantro and serve. You can add 1 tablespoon of ghee, if you wish.

Instant Pot Sultani Dal

Servings: 4

Ingredients

Main ingredients:

300g toor dal

A handful of cilantro

½ teaspoon of turmeric

2 cups + 3 tablespoons water

1 cup toor dal

1 teaspoon of sugar

2 teaspoons salt

1 tablespoon of ghee or oil

1 tablespoon of butter

Generous pinch of saffron

2 tablespoons yogurt

1 tablespoon of cream

½ cup of milk

½ teaspoon of cumin seeds

1 inch cinnamon

2 cardamoms

3 cloves

2 green chilies

2 garlic cloves

1 onion

Directions

1. Cut the cilantro and the onion. Set aside.

2. Slice the green chili and then chop the garlic.

3. Mix together the saffron and 3 tablespoons of water. Set aside.

4. Carefully wash the toor dal and add it to your Instant Pot. Add the turmeric powder and 2 cups of water. Select the Manual mode and set the time for 7 minutes. Once done, allow for natural pressure release.

5. Once the pressure has been released, open the lid and mash the dal. Remove. Set aside.

6. Select the Sauté mode on your Instant Pot and add the butter and the ghee. Once the butter melts, add the cloves, cumin seeds, green cardamom, and cinnamon. Cook for 1

minute. Add the onion, green chili, and garlic. Sauté until the onion is translucent.

7. Add the cooked and mashed dal and season with salt. Mix the ingredients thoroughly.

8. Add milk and yogurt. Mix together. Cover with a glass lid. Cook for 2 to 3 minutes.

9. Add the saffron and water from the saffron. Simmer for 1 minute.

10. Add the cream. Let it come to a boil. Keep warm until ready to serve.

In the following chapter, we will look at some chicken recipes that you can prepare in your Instant Pot.

Chapter 6: Instant Pot Chicken Recipes

Glossary Of Terms You Will Find In This Chapter

Korma: Any Indian dish that contains cream or meat or vegetables that are braised with yogurt, stock, and water.

Kashmiri chili powder: A spice that is relatively mild in heat and full of flavor. It is similar to paprika.

Saag: Common leafy green vegetables that are found in India. When people mention saag, they mostly are talking about dill, collard greens, spinach, and other vegetables.

Garam masala: A combination of ground spices that are blended together.

Ghee: Clarified butter, which you can find in an Indian store. If you cannot find this item, substitute it with butter or any oil of your choice.

Serrano peppers: Capsicum annum, which is a type of chili pepper that comes from Mexico.

Coconut aminos: Sauce that is made of coconut sap. It usually resembles soy sauce as it is dark, salty, and at the same time slightly sweet. If you cannot find coconut aminos, you can replace it with soy sauce.

Trivet: A three-legged metal stand that is placed over a fire for a kettle or a cooking pot to stand on.

Chicken Korma

Servings: 3

Ingredients

1 ½ pounds of chicken thighs, cut into pieces (or about 6 skinless drumsticks)

1 teaspoon salt

½ cup full-fat or Greek yogurt

1 teaspoon of cumin powder

1 teaspoon of coriander powder

½ to 1 teaspoon of Kashmiri chili powder or any mild red chili powder

¼ teaspoon of turmeric

1 teaspoon of garlic cloves, minced

1 teaspoon of ginger, minced

1 large onion, finely chopped

½ teaspoon of cumin seeds

12 black peppers

4 cloves

4 green cardamoms, whole

1 tablespoon of cooking oil

Chopped cilantro, for garnish

Directions

1. Select the Sauté mode on your Instant Pot. Wait for the pot to become hot and then add the oil. Add the cardamom, black pepper, cloves, and cumin. Cook for 30 seconds.

2. Add the onion and stir to mix well. Cook for 2 minutes. You should cover the pot with a glass lid.

3. Add the ginger, coriander powder, turmeric, cumin powder, red chili powder, and salt. Stir to combine.

4. Add the chicken and coat it evenly with the spices. Add ¼ cup of water. Close the lid and make sure the valve is in the Sealing position. Set the time for 8 minutes on Manual High pressure. Once done, let the pressure release naturally for 5 minutes.

5. Open the lid and mix some spoonful of hot curry with yogurt. Cook for a few minutes on the Sauté mode. This will allow the sauce to thicken.

6. Garnish with cilantro and serve.

Instant Pot Saag Chicken

Servings: 4

Ingredients

2 tablespoons fresh lime juice

1 cup packed very finely chopped spinach

1 cup kale, finely chopped (you can use a food processor for very fresh kale)

½ cup diced tomatoes

1 large stick (about 2 inches) cinnamon, broken into pieces

1 ½ teaspoons salt

1 teaspoon of cayenne pepper

1 teaspoon of turmeric

1 ½ pounds, boneless, skinless chicken thighs cut into smaller pieces

1 tablespoon freshly grated ginger

1 red onion, diced

1 teaspoon of whole cumin seeds

2 tablespoons oil

Chopped cilantro to garnish

Directions

1. Select the Sauté function on your Instant Pot and proceed to heat the oil. Once the oil is hot, add the cumin seeds and allow them to start sizzling.

2. Add the red onion and then add the ginger. Cook for about 5 minutes or until the onion becomes soft and translucent.

3. Add the chicken thighs, cayenne pepper, turmeric, and salt. Stir to mix well. Add the cinnamon. Stir again.

4. Add the tomatoes, spinach, and kale. Cover with the lid and then set the time for 12 minutes on the Pressure Cook option.

5. Once cooking is complete, allow the Instant Pot to release the pressure naturally.

6. Open the lid carefully and add the lime juice. Stir to incorporate it.

7. Garnish the saag chicken with cilantro. Serve.

Instant Pot Chicken and Potato Curry

Servings: 6

Ingredients

1 to 2 tablespoons butter, optional

1 (15-ounces) can reduced fat coconut milk

2 (15-ounces) cans canned tomato sauce

½ teaspoon paprika

1 teaspoon of salt (I use coarse kosher salt)

2 teaspoons turmeric

2 teaspoons garam masala

2 teaspoons ground coriander

2 cups peeled, chopped russet yellow or red potatoes (about 10 ounces)

2 lbs. boneless, skinless chicken breasts, cut into 1-inch pieces

½ tablespoon grated fresh ginger or ginger paste

3 to 4 medium cloves garlic, finely minced or pressed (about 2 teaspoons)

½ cup diced white, red or yellow onions

1 tablespoon of ghee, cooking oil, or butter

Fresh, chopped cilantro, for garnish

Hot, cooked rice for serving

Directions

1. Press the Sauté function and adjust the temperature to Normal (using the + or − button). Add the oil and heat it. Once the oil is hot, add the onions. Cook for 2 to 3 minutes, making sure you stir; the onions should turn translucent. Add the ginger and the garlic. Cook for 10 to 20 more seconds.

2. Add the chicken and cook for 1 to 2 minutes. Make sure you stir the chicken frequently.

3. Add the potatoes, paprika, coriander, turmeric, garam masala, salt, coconut milk, and tomato sauce. Stir well to combine all the ingredients.

4. Close the lid well and make sure that the valve is closed. Select 6 minutes on the Manual or Pressure Cook setting.

5. Once the beep sounds, do a quick release. If you notice any bubbling or spurting, close

the valve and allow the food to sit for 10 minutes before trying to open again. Remove the lid.

6. Add the butter and stir well to allow the butter to melt completely.

7. Garnish with fresh cilantro and serve with rice, if you wish.

Indian Chicken Curry with Milk

Servings: 4

Ingredients

1 ½ cups crushed tomatoes, canned

1 tablespoon garlic, minced

½ tablespoon ginger, minced

2 Serrano peppers, diced

1 cup onion, diced

1 ½ pounds boneless skinless chicken breasts cut into 1-inch pieces

3 tablespoons canola oil

1 handful cilantro, chopped

½ cup full fat milk (3.25% or more)

2 bay leaves

½ teaspoon cayenne pepper

1 teaspoon of garam masala

1 teaspoon of paprika

¼ teaspoon turmeric, ground

1 teaspoon cumin, ground

Directions

1. Prepare all the ground spices. Set aside.

2. Season the chicken with kosher salt.

3. Press the Sauté Normal function on your Instant Pot and add the oil. Once the oil starts shimmering, add the chicken and cook on all sides. This should take about 4 minutes. Once done, remove it. Set aside. Turn off the Sauté function.

4. Adjust to Sauté (-) option and then add 2 tablespoons of canola oil. Once the oil is hot, cook the onion for 4 minutes. Add the chili, ginger, and spices and cook for 2 more minutes. Add the garlic and proceed to cook for 30 more seconds or until fragrant. Make sure you stir the ingredients well.

5. Add ½ cup of water to deglaze the pot. You can use a wooden spoon to scrape off any sticky brown bits.

6. Add the crushed tomatoes and stir the chicken. Cook for 1 minute.

7. Close the lid and set the time for 2 minutes on Manual High pressure. Once done, allow for natural pressure release. This should

take 10 minutes. Once done, manually release any remaining pressure.

8. Temper the milk. You can remove some of the sauce before adding it a little at a time to the milk. Stir the mixture thoroughly. Add it to your Instant Pot. Stir to combine.

9. Remove the bay leaves and then garnish the curry with cilantro. You can serve over rice, if you wish.

Instant Pot Chicken Tikka Masala

Servings: 4

Ingredients

½ cup canned coconut milk

½ cup chicken broth

1 ½ pounds boneless skinless chicken breast

1 (14-ounce) can diced tomatoes with juice

¼ teaspoon cayenne pepper, optional

1 teaspoon of ground coriander

2 teaspoons cumin seeds

1 teaspoon of ground turmeric

1 teaspoon of garam masala

2 teaspoons paprika

1 (1-inch) piece of ginger, peeled and chopped

3 cloves garlic, minced

1 small onion, chopped

2 tablespoons cooking oil

Chopped fresh basil or cilantro, optional

1 tablespoon of arrowroot starch, optional

Juice of 1 lemon

Directions

1. Select the Sauté function on your Instant Pot and then turn to High heat. Wait for the pot to get hot and then add the cooking oil. Add the onion, ginger, garlic and sauté for 3 to 4 minutes. Stir the ingredients frequently, until the onions turn translucent.

2. Press Cancel and add the spices. Use a wooden spoon to scrape off any bits at the bottom of the pot. Add the tomatoes, stir well, and then arrange the chicken on top. Pour the chicken broth into the pot and close the lid properly.

3. Set the time for 7 minutes on Manual High pressure.

4. Once cooking is done, do a quick release. Carefully remove the lid and use a fork to break up the chicken and then put it back into your Instant Pot.

5. Press the Sauté function and simmer the chicken for 4 to 5 more minutes. Add the coconut milk and stir. If the consistency is too thin, you can mix the lemon juice and arrowroot starch and pour the mixture into

your Instant Pot. Taste and adjust seasoning.

6. Once the sauce is thick, remove and garnish with cilantro or fresh basil.

7. Serve immediately.

Instant Pot Spiced Roast Chicken

Servings: 4

Ingredients

1 ½ cups chicken broth or stock

1 tablespoon coconut oil

1 whole (3 to 5 lbs.) chicken

3 medium limes

3 fluid ounces coconut milk, canned

2 teaspoons sea salt

1 tablespoon of chili powder

1 teaspoon of honey, raw

2 tablespoons coconut aminos (or soy sauce if you cannot find coconut aminos)

¾ teaspoon coriander, ground

1 teaspoon of cumin seeds

1 ounce tomato paste

1 tablespoon peeled and minced fresh ginger

4 teaspoons minced garlic cloves

1 teaspoon of cayenne pepper

3 tablespoons diced shallot

Directions

1. Add shallot, coriander, cayenne pepper, cumin, garlic cloves, coconut aminos, ginger, honey, tomato paste, sea salt, chili powder, and coconut milk into a blender. Pulse the ingredients until they form a paste.

2. Prepare the chicken and remove the innards. Use half of the paste to carefully cover the outside parts of the chicken and squeeze the lime juice on the chicken. Place the remaining paste as well as the line rinds inside the chicken.

3. Select the Sauté function and heat the coconut oil.

4. Add the chicken. The breast side should be down. Cook for 3 to 4 minutes and then flip it and cook the other side.

5. Remove the chicken and place the trivet inside your Instant Pot. Carefully put the chicken on the trivet with the breast side facing up. Spread the broth all over the chicken.

6. Close the lid and make sure the valve is set to Sealing. Set the time for 25 minutes on High pressure. Once time is up, allow the pressure to release naturally.

7. Serve and enjoy.

Mango Chicken Curry

Servings: 6

Ingredients

3 pounds chicken thighs, boneless, skinless

½ cup cilantro chopped

Juice from ½ lime

3 cups of baby spinach

2 cups of frozen mango pieces

1 (400 ml) can of coconut milk

1 cup chicken stock

2 medium sweet potatoes largely diced

½ head cauliflower (about 4 cups), cut in large pieces

½ teaspoon paprika

½ teaspoon of cayenne

1 teaspoon of turmeric

2 teaspoons of cumin seeds

2 teaspoons curry powder

2 teaspoons kosher salt

3 tablespoons tomato paste

1 teaspoon minced ginger or 2 teaspoons ground ginger

3 teaspoons minced garlic cloves or 2 teaspoons garlic powder

1 medium onion, diced

2 tablespoons ghee or neutral oil, such as avocado oil

Directions

1. Select the Sauté function on your Instant Pot.

2. Once the pot is hot, add the ghee, turmeric, onion, ginger, garlic, cumin, salt, tomato paste, cayenne, curry powder, and paprika. Cook for 3 minutes or until fragrant. The onions should be softened.

3. Add the chicken thighs, cauliflower, and sweet potato. Stir well to coat the ingredients with the spices.

4. Add the coconut milk and the chicken broth. Stir to combine.

5. Cancel the Sauté function and cover the pot. Lock properly for pressure cooking.

6. Set the time for 20 minutes on Manual High pressure.

7. After the time is up, proceed to do a quick release.

8. Add the baby spinach, lime juice, and frozen mango. Stir well to combine.

9. Allow the curry to sit for 10 minutes.

10. Remove and garnish with cilantro. Serve.

Instant Pot Butter Chicken

Servings: 6

Ingredients

3 chicken breasts (about 1.5 lbs. total), cut into 1 inch cubes

1 teaspoon of garam masala

1 teaspoon of cumin seeds

1 teaspoon of salt

1 teaspoon of turmeric

1 teaspoon of paprika

2 teaspoon minced ginger (you can use the paste)

2 tablespoons minced garlic cloves (you can use garlic paste)

¼ cup chicken broth

14.5 ounce can diced tomatoes

To Finish:

Fresh cilantro for garnish

1 teaspoon of garam masala

¼ cup unsweetened coconut milk

¼ cup heavy cream

¼ cup butter

Directions

1. Add the tomatoes, spices, and the broth into the Instant Pot. Stir well to combine.

2. Add the chicken and proceed to stir once more. Try to coat the chicken as much as you can.

3. Close the lid and make sure the valve is in Sealing position.

4. Select 6 minutes on Manual High pressure.

5. Once the time is up, allow for natural pressure release. This should take 5 minutes. Once ready, do a quick release.

6. Open the lid carefully and remove the chicken. Try to leave most of the tomatoes inside your pot.

7. Use an immersion blender to blend the broth, spices, and tomatoes. Add the butter, milk, garam masala, and cream. Stir well until incorporated.

8. Place the chicken back into your pot. Cook until heated through.

9. Serve and enjoy.

Chapter 7: Instant Pot Vegetarian Recipes

Glossary Of Terms You Will Find In This Chapter

Aloo Gobi: A dry Indian dish made of potatoes, cauliflower, and spices.

Amchoor: A mango powder that Indians use to add a sour tangy fruity flavor.

Asafoetida: A brownish gum that comes from various plants. It has a strong taste and odor.

Chal Dal: A sauce that is made of lentils and spices. It is mostly served with rice.

Chana: Hindi name for chickpea or garbanzo beans.

Chana dal: Chickpeas or garbanzo beans.

Dal: Dried split pulses, such as beans, peas, and lentils as well as the different soups that are made using these pulses. Horse gram and other beans, peas, and lentils belong to this category.

Dosa: A pancake that is made from ground pulses and rice flour. It is mostly served with some spiced vegetable filling.

Garam masala: A combination of ground spices.

Hing: The English word for hing is asafetida (also spelled without an "o" as asafetida). It is a sticky liquid that has a strong smell. It comes from the roots of plants.

Horse gram: A type of beans, which is mostly found in the southern parts of India. It is rich in such nutrients as iron, protein, calcium, and phosphorus. You can think of horse gram as "brown lentils."

Idli: Savory rice cake

Kasuri methi: A semi-arid crop that is cultivated worldwide. Its leaves consist of three tiny obviate to almost oblong leaflets. Indians usually use its seeds in their ingredients.

Keema Matar: An Indian dish that consists of minced meat and pea.

Moong dal: Indian name for skinned and split mung beans.

Naan: A type of leavened bread that looks like pita bread. It is made of wheat flour and baked in a tandoori oven. It is usually roughly triangular in shape and forms crispy spots which come from bubbles that form in the hot clay oven.

Palek paneer: A vegetable dish that is made from a thick paste made of paneer (it is a non-melting fresh cheese made with lemon juice and curdling heated milk) and puréed spinach which is seasoned with garam masala, garlic, and other spices. Paneer has the consistency of some types of tofu.

Roti: An Indian name for a flat round bread that is normally cooked on a griddle.

Sambar: A dish that consists of vegetables and lentils cooked with tamarind and other spices.

Vankaya Kothimeera Kaaram: Indian term for eggplant in cilantro gravy.

Tikka masala: Indian style dish that consists of small pieces of meat (mostly chicken) that combine with a creamy sauce that is flavored with spices.

Tofu: Bean curd.

Instant Pot Kale Stew

Servings: 4

Ingredients

1 ½ teaspoons of salt

4 cups of water

4 teaspoons of turmeric

¼ cup of cilantro

¾ teaspoon of red chili powder

1 ½ teaspoons of coriander powder

1 teaspoon of cumin seeds

1 teaspoon of oil

1 clove of garlic

½ cup horse gram or brown dal or lentils

3 tomatoes

4 (1/3 cup) green onions

3 cups tightly packed kale

Directions

1. Soak the dal for 8 to 10 hours. Drain. Add ½ cup of water and 1 garlic clove and grind into a paste.

2. Chop the kale, green onions, and the tomatoes. Set aside.

3. Select the Sauté function on your Instant Pot. Add the oil.

4. Once the oil is hot, proceed to add the cumin seeds and let them splutter. Add the tomatoes. Sauté for 1 minute.

5. Add the green onions, chopped kale, coriander powder, turmeric powder, salt, and red chili powder. Stir to combine well.

6. Cover the Instant Pot and use the steam mode on your Instant Pot to cook.

7. Once the kale wilts, add the ground horse gram dal, and pour in 2 cups of water. Stir to combine.

8. Cook for 5 minutes at Manual High pressure ensuring you stir frequently. This will keep the dal from browning up. Add the cilantro and the remaining water after 3 to 4 minutes. Once ready, quick release the pressure.

9. Serve hot with rice, if you wish.

Instant Pot Palek Paneer

Servings: 2 to 4

Ingredients

1 medium finely chopped tomato

Cream or cashew paste to garnish

14 ounce of paneer cubes

½ cup water or as needed

400 to 500 grams spinach

1 tablespoon of ginger-garlic paste

1 green chili slit into pieces

½ finely chopped onion

2 to 3 tablespoons ghee, butter, or oil

Spices

2 teaspoons garam masala

Salt to taste

Red chili powder to taste

1 ½ tablespoons coriander powder

1 tablespoon of cumin seeds

Directions

134

1. Select the Sauté High mode on your Instant Pot.

2. Add the ghee. Allow it to get hot. Add the cumin seeds. Fry them well.

3. Add the onions and the green chili. Cook until the onions are fragrant and turn translucent.

4. Add the tomatoes and fry them until they become mushy.

5. Add the spice powders and season with salt. Mix well to combine.

6. Add the spinach and stir to combine. Turn off the Sauté mode.

7. Close the lid and make sure the vent is in the Sealing position.

8. Select 2 minutes on Manual High pressure. Once cooking is done, allow the food to stay in the keep warm mode for 2 minutes and then proceed to do a quick release.

9. Grind the mixture together using a hand blender. It should become a fine paste. You can add more water if needed and cook for 5 minutes on Sauté High mode.

10. Add the garam masala and mix well.

11. Add the paneer cubes and simmer for 2 to 4 minutes.

12. Serve with cashew paste or cream, if you wish.

Eggplant Curry (Vankaya Kothimeera Kaaram)

Servings: 4 to 6

Ingredients

¼ cup of water or as needed

2 tablespoons of oil

½ tablespoon mustard seeds

½ tablespoon cumin seeds

15 eggplants

To grind:

1 inch sized ball tamarind

1 inch piece ginger

Salt to taste

Green chili to taste

1 bunch fresh cilantro

Directions

1. Grind the tamarind, ginger, cilantro, green chili, and salt. You should use little or no water when grinding.

2. Carefully wash the eggplants and create criss-cross slits to about ¾ length of the eggplants.

3. Carefully stuff the cilantro paste into the slits you created. Set aside.

4. Select the Sauté High mode and heat the oil.

5. Once the oil is shimmering, add the mustard seeds and cumin seeds and fry them.

6. Turn off the Sauté function.

7. Arrange the stuffed eggplants in a layer in your Instant Pot. Spread the remaining cilantro paste on top. Add ¼ cup of water.

8. Mix gently if you wish or leave it as is.

9. Close the lid and make sure the vent is in the Sealing position.

10. Set the time for 5 minutes on Manual Low pressure.

11. Once time is up, allow it to stay in the warm mode for 2 minutes before doing a quick release.

12. Remove and serve with rice and ghee, if you wish.

Chal Dal Veggie Soup

Servings: 2

Ingredients

1 ½ cups or more veggies, chopped small (you can use small cauliflower florets, sliced carrots, and cubed butternut squash)

2 juicy tomatoes or 1 ¼ cups puréed tomatoes

¼ to ½ teaspoon cayenne

1 teaspoon of turmeric

1 teaspoon of garam masala or use ½ teaspoon cumin + ½ teaspoon coriander

½ inch ginger, finely chopped

5 cloves of garlic, chopped

½ medium onion, chopped

1 teaspoon of oil

3 cups water

½ cup washed split chickpeas or yellow split peas (preferably soaked for half an hour)

Cilantro and lemon for garnish

¾ teaspoon or more salt

Directions

1. Press the Sauté function on your Instant Pot and heat the oil. Add onion and garlic. Sauté for 5 minutes.

2. Add the spices and stir to mix in then sauté for 1 minute.

3. Add the puréed tomato and the veggies and stir to combine; sauté for a few minutes until soft. Transfer these contents to a bowl.

4. Add the split peas or chana dal and ½ to 1 cup of water into your Instant Pot. Season with salt. Stir to combine. Cook at Manual High for 6 to 7 minutes.

5. Quick release pressure and then add the contents you had set aside in a bowl, stir, and adjust seasoning, if necessary.

6. Remove and garnish with cilantro. You can serve with rice, pita bread, or flat bread or as a soup, if you wish.

Instant Pot Chana Dal

Servings: 3

Ingredients

½ teaspoon garam masala

¼ teaspoon red chili powder or cayenne pepper

¼ + 1/8 teaspoon turmeric powder

¾ teaspoon salt

1 ½ to 2 cups water

1 tomato

¾ cup chana dal (split garbanzo beans or chick peas), rinsed

Tempering:

1 tablespoon chopped cilantro, for garnish

1 to 2 teaspoons lemon juice, more or less depending on taste

¼ teaspoon mustard seeds

½ teaspoon cumin seeds

2 dried red chilies

Pinch of hing or asafoetida (also spelled as asafetida)

2 garlic cloves

2 teaspoons oil

Directions

1. Add the chana dal, garam masala, tomato, turmeric powder, red chili powder, salt, and water into your Instant Pot.

2. Close the lid well and make sure the valve is set to Sealing. Select 12 minutes on Manual High pressure. Once done, allow for natural pressure release. Alternatively, soak the chana dal for at least 1 hour. If you do so, you'll only need to set time for 7 to 8 minutes on Manual High pressure.

3. Open the lid carefully and stir the ingredients. Press Cancel and select the Sauté option.

4. In the meantime, sauté some mustard seeds and cumin in a pan. Add the red chilies, asafoetida (hing), and chopped garlic. If you want extra spice, you should split the red chilies into two. Sauté until the garlic is golden brown. Add the tempering to your

Instant Pot and stir well. You can use a
spoon to mash some of the dal.

5. Garnish with cilantro and lemon juice.
Serve with rice.

Instant Pot Chana Masala

Servings: 4

Ingredients

¼ cup of cilantro

2 cups Instant Pot chickpeas or canned chickpeas

2 cups water

1 teaspoon of garam masala

1 teaspoon of brown sugar

1 teaspoon of salt

1 teaspoon Indian mango powder

2 teaspoons coriander powder

1 teaspoon freshly ground black pepper

½ to 1 teaspoon Indian red chili powder or cayenne pepper

½ teaspoon of turmeric powder

1 (8 oz.) can tomato sauce

1 chopped jalapeño pepper, optional

2 teaspoons ginger, minced

1 tablespoon garlic, minced

1½ cups onion, finely chopped

1 teaspoon of cumin seeds

2 tablespoons ghee, butter, or oil

Naan or basmati rice for serving, optional

Directions

1. Select the Sauté function and choose 'Normal' temperature.

2. Heat the oil or ghee and then cook the cumin seeds for 10 seconds or until fragrant.

3. Add the onions, ginger, garlic, and jalapeño pepper and cook for 7 minutes. The onions should turn golden brown but be careful not to burn them.

4. Add the tomato sauce. Cook for 5 minutes as you stir frequently. The tomato mixture should look like a paste.

5. Add the turmeric, amchoor, chili powder, brown sugar, coriander, black pepper, garam masala, and salt. Cook for 30 seconds, while stirring frequently.

6. Use water to deglaze the pot; you can use a wooden stick to scrape off any sticky bits on the bottom.

7. Add the chickpeas and then stir to combine.

8. Set the time for 6 minutes on the Manual mode.

9. Once cooking is complete, let the pressure release naturally.

10. Open the lid and then stir in the chana masala. You can sauté for a few minutes, if you wish for thicker gravy. Top with 1 teaspoon of ghee and cilantro, if you wish.

11. Serve with basmati rice or naan.

Moong Dal Sambar

Servings: 2

Ingredients

½ cup yellow split moong dal

1 cup of any vegetable, optional

Salt to taste

1 tablespoon of chili powder or 1 green chili

1 ½ cups of water

1 tablespoon of oil

¼ teaspoon Asafoetida

5 cloves garlic

10 leaves curry

½ tablespoon mustard seeds

1 tablespoon of cumin seeds

Directions

1. Press the Sauté function on your Instant Pot. Once the pot is hot, cook the moong dal for 2 to 3 minutes or until golden brown. Set aside.

2. Add some oil to your Instant Pot. Allow it to get hot and then add the asafoetida and mustard seeds.

3. Wait for the mustard seeds to pop and then add the garlic, cumin seeds, and curry leaves. Cook for 1 minute.

4. Add the remaining ingredients plus the water and close the lid properly.

5. Cancel the Sauté function and then set the time for 15 minutes on the Manual mode.

6. Once done, let the pressure release. Once the sambar cools down, mash it well to combine the ingredients.

7. Serve with rice, dosa, idli, or roti, if you wish.

Vegan Curried Butternut Squash Soup

Servings: 4

Ingredients

½ cup of coconut milk (or coconut cream)

3 cups of water

1 ½ teaspoons of fine sea salt

1 (3 pound) butternut squash that has been peeled then cut into 1-inch cubes

1 tablespoon of curry powder

2 cloves garlic, minced

1 large onion, chopped

1 teaspoon of extra-virgin cooking oil

Optional Toppings: Dried cranberries and hulled pumpkin seeds

Directions

1. Select the Sauté function on your Instant Pot. Add the cooking oil once the pot is hot. Add the onion and cook for about 8 minutes or until tender. Add the curry powder and garlic and cook for 1 minute or until fragrant.

149

2. Turn your Instant Pot off then add the butternut squash, water, and salt. Cover the pot with the lid and make sure the valve is set to Sealing. Press the 'Soup' option and allow the soup to cook for 30 minutes at High pressure.

3. Once cooking is complete, you can wait for natural pressure release. This should take 10 minutes; or, you can do a quick release.

4. Once the pressure is released, open the lid. Purée the soup using an immersion blender. Alternatively, you can pulse it in a blender or food processor. Be careful when using the blender, as hot liquids tend to blow off the lid. You can use a dishtowel to cover the vent of your blender instead of using a lid.

5. Place the puréed soup in your Instant Pot and then add the coconut milk. Stir well to combine. You can adjust the seasoning, if needed.

6. Add dried cranberries or hulled seeds to top, if you wish.

7. Serve and enjoy. You can refrigerate the leftovers for up to 1 week in an airtight container.

Aloo Gobi

Servings: 4 to 6

Ingredients

½ teaspoon garam masala

1 teaspoon roasted cumin powder

1 to 2 teaspoons coriander powder

¼ to ½ teaspoon cayenne

½ teaspoon turmeric powder

1 teaspoon of salt

1 medium tomato, chopped

1 teaspoon ginger, finely chopped

1 teaspoon garlic, finely chopped

2 cups cauliflower florets

1 cup Yukon gold potatoes, sliced (red potatoes can work too)

2 to 4 green chilies or 2 jalapeños (de-seeded for milder flavor)

½ cup onion, sliced

1 teaspoon of cumin seeds

1 tablespoon of ghee, butter, or oil

2 tablespoons chopped cilantro for garnish

Directions

1. Press the Sauté function on your Instant Pot and wait for it to display 'Hot'. Add the cumin seeds and allow them to sizzle. Add the onions, potatoes, and green chilies. Cook for 1 minute. Add the chopped ginger-garlic. Cook for 1 more minute.

2. Add the chopped tomato, spices, and salt and cook for 2 minutes. Add the cauliflower florets. Stir gently.

3. Cancel the Sauté mode and make sure the valve is in the Sealing position. Select 0-1 minutes on the Manual setting. The time will depend on the size of the potato and florets.

4. Do Manual pressure release and then open the lid. You can sauté for a few minutes if there is liquid left in the pot.

5. Garnish with cilantro. Serve.

Instant Pot Cauliflower Tikka Masala

Servings: 4

Ingredients

½ cup non-dairy yogurt (or cashew cream)

1 cauliflower head, cut into florets

1 tablespoon of maple syrup

1 (28-ounce) can crushed or diced tomatoes

½ teaspoon salt

¼ teaspoon ground cumin

½ teaspoon ground chili

1 teaspoon of turmeric

2 teaspoons of garam masala

2 teaspoons of dried fenugreek leaves

1 tablespoon of freshly grated ginger

3 cloves of garlic, minced

1 medium onion, diced

1 tablespoon of vegan butter (or cooking oil of your choice)

Optional toppings: Roasted cashews and fresh parsley

Directions

1. Select the Sauté function and set time for 7 minutes. Add the oil and allow it to get hot. Add the onion, ginger, and garlic and sauté for 3 to 4 minutes. The onions should be soft and caramelized. Add the cumin, fenugreek leaves, turmeric, chili, garam masala, salt and sauté for 2 more minutes. Stir frequently to prevent the ingredients from burning. The Instant Pot should have now turned off.

2. Add the tomatoes, cauliflower florets, and the maple syrup and close the lid well. Make sure the vent is in the Sealing position. Set the time for 2 minutes on the Pressure Cook option.

3. Once cooking is done, wait 1 minute and then release the pressure. Add the non-dairy yogurt and stir well to combine.

4. Serve hot with naan, rice, or tofu. You can top with roasted cashews and fresh parsley, if you wish.

Instant Pot Lentil and Spinach Dal

Servings: 6

Ingredients

1 ½ cups of red lentils or yellow split peas (or a combination of both)

Cooked brown rice or naan

Fresh cilantro

Plain yogurt

2 teaspoon of butter, optional

¼ cup of chopped fresh cilantro, optional

Several big handfuls of spinach (about 4 cups)

1 large tomato, cut into 6-8 wedges

½ teaspoon of salt

3 cups water

¼ teaspoon dried cayenne pepper

1 teaspoon of ground turmeric

1 teaspoon of ground coriander

1 teaspoon of ground cumin

3 cloves garlic, minced

1 large onion (red or yellow), chopped

2 tablespoons coconut or cooking oil

Directions

1. Press the Sauté function and set the heat to medium. Once the pot is hot, add the cooking oil or coconut oil and allow it to get hot. Add the onions and sauté until they turn soft and become translucent. Add the garlic and stir. Sauté for 1 more minute or until fragrant. Press the Cancel button. Add the cayenne, cumin, turmeric, and coriander. Stir to mix well.

2. Add the lentils, tomato wedges, salt, and water. Stir well. Cover the pot and make sure the valve is in the Sealing position. Set the time for 10 minutes on the Manual setting.

3. Once cooking is complete, press Cancel and let it sit for 10 minutes. Open the valve to allow the pressure to release.

4. Carefully remove the tomato skins and discard them. Whisk the lentils and smash the tomatoes.

5. Add the spinach, butter, and cilantro. Stir well to combine. The residual heat will be enough to wilt the spinach.

6. Serve with naan or brown rice. You can top with fresh cilantro and yogurt, if you wish.

Keema Matar

Ingredients

¾ cup water to be added in 2 parts

3 tablespoons tomato paste

1 teaspoon of paprika

½ teaspoon red chili powder

1 teaspoons ground cumin

3 teaspoons coriander powder

2 teaspoons garam masala

½ teaspoon turmeric powder

1 teaspoon of salt

1 small onion, fine chopped

1 tablespoon ginger-garlic paste (3 cloves garlic + ½ inch ginger)

2 tablespoons cooking oil

¾ to 1 cup frozen peas

1 pound ground meat (chicken, turkey, lamb, or beef)

Directions

1. Finely chop the onion and ginger-garlic paste. Set aside. Press the Sauté function on the Instant Pot and allow the pot to warm up. This should take 30 seconds. Add the oil and then add the onions and ginger-garlic paste. Cook for 1 minute.

2. Add the dry spices and season with salt. Cook for 30 seconds. Add 3 tablespoons of tomato paste and then pour in ¼ cup of water. The water will allow you to stir the ingredients easily. Stir well and cook for 30 seconds.

3. Add the ground meat and ½ cup of water. Stir to incorporate the spices with the meat. You can use a wooden spoon to break up the meat. Mix well.

4. Close the lid and make sure the valve is set to Sealing. Set the time for 10 minutes on the Manual setting. After cooking is done, release the pressure manually. If you'll be using ground turkey or chicken, you should set the cooking time to 8 minutes.

5. Carefully open the lid and press the Sauté function. Add the fresh or frozen peas to

cook through. Once done, turn off the Instant Pot.

6. Add some fresh cilantro and stir.

7. Serve and enjoy.

Instant Pot Black Eyed Peas

Servings: 3

Ingredients

For the Black Eyed Peas Curry Recipe:

1 teaspoon of kasuri methi (dried fenugreek leaves)

½ teaspoon of garam masala

2 ¼ cups of water

1 cup black eyed peas (lobia)

1 teaspoon of coriander powder

1 teaspoon of red chili powder

½ teaspoon of turmeric powder

Salt

1 teaspoon of cumin seeds

2 tablespoons oil

For paste:

1 green chili

2 cloves garlic

1 inch ginger

3 medium tomatoes

1 small or ½ cup onion

Directions

1. In a food processor, prepare the paste ingredients. You can have a smooth or coarse paste, as you wish.

2. Wash and drain the beans. Set aside.

3. Select the Sauté function on your Instant Pot and let the pot get hot. Add the oil and the cumin seeds. Allow the seeds to sizzle.

4. Add the paste. Cook until it forms a thick paste; the water should evaporate.

5. Add the red chili powder, salt, and coriander powder. Cook for 1 minute.

6. Add the beans and the water.

7. Close the lid properly and make sure the vent is in the Sealing position. Set the time for 18 minutes on Manual High pressure. Let the pressure release.

8. Open the lid, add the kasuri methi and garam masala. Mix well.

9. Garnish with cilantro and then serve.

We will now look at other tasty recipes that you can prepare in your Instant Pot.

Chapter 8: Other Recipes

Glossary Of Terms You Will Find In This Chapter

Garam masala: A combination of ground spices

Pavbhaji: Bread curry. It is a fast food made with toasted bread roll and a thick vegetable curry.

Besan: Gram flour that is made from chickpeas. It is mostly used to flavor chicken curries. It is also used to make pancakes, bhajias, and steamed patties.

Kadhi: Indian gravy that is made of yogurt, vegetable fritters, and chickpea flour.

Raita: An Indian condiment or salad that is made of vegetables, fruits, spices, herbs, and yogurt curds.

Halwa: This refers to a sweet pudding dessert.

Arborio rice: Italian short-grain rice. It is usually starchy, creamy, and chewy when cooked.

Sabzi: Vegetables cooked in gravy.

Seviyan: An Indian dessert that looks like spaghetti.

Kesar: Saffron. It is an orange-yellow colored natural food flavoring which also serves as a food color.

Elaichi: Cardamom.

Idli: A type of savory rice cake.

Instant Pot Indian Spiced Sauce

Servings: 2

Ingredients

1 cup of water

1 (28-ounce) can of whole tomatoes and their liquid (fire-roasted optional)

1 tablespoon of garam masala

1 tablespoon of sweet paprika

1 teaspoon of ground turmeric

¾ teaspoon cayenne pepper

1 tablespoon of ground cumin

1 tablespoon of ground coriander

¾ teaspoon of fine-grain sea salt, plus more to taste

1-inch knob fresh ginger, peeled and grated

3 cloves garlic, finely chopped

3 large onions, finely diced

2 tablespoons cooking oil

Directions

1. Select the Sauté function on your Instant Pot and heat the oil. Once the oil is hot, add the onions, ginger, garlic, and salt. Sauté for about 10 minutes. The onion should be soft and translucent.

2. Add the coriander, paprika, cumin, garam masala, turmeric, and cayenne. Stir. Sauté for 1 minute before adding the tomatoes along with their liquid. You can use your hands to break up and crush the tomatoes before adding them to the Instant Pot. Stir well to combine. Add the water and stir.

3. Close and secure the lid. The pressure release valve should be in the Sealing position. Press Cancel and then set the time for 15 minutes on Manual High pressure.

4. Once cooking is complete, allow for 10 minutes natural pressure release and then proceed do a quick release.

5. Serve the sauce immediately or refrigerate for a few days, if you wish.

Chicken Tikka with Cauliflower and Peas

Servings: 6

Ingredients

½ full fat canned coconut milk

½ cup frozen peas

2 cups of cauliflower florets

14 ounce can of diced tomatoes, drained

¼ teaspoon ground cardamom

¼ teaspoon cayenne pepper

½ garam masala

½ teaspoon turmeric

1 teaspoon of cumin seeds

1 teaspoon of ground coriander

1 teaspoon grated ginger root

3 cloves garlic, minced

½ chopped onion

½ tablespoon ghee, butter or coconut oil for frying

1 ½ teaspoons of kosher salt

1 ½ pounds of skinless, boneless chicken thighs, cubed

¼ cup fresh cilantro leaves, for serving

Directions

1. Season the chicken well with 1 teaspoon salt.

2. Select the Sauté function on your Instant Pot and melt the butter. Add the onions, spices, garlic, and ginger. Cook for 2 to 3 minutes. The vegetables should be soft and the spices should be fragrant.

3. Add the tomatoes and purée using an immersion blender. Alternatively, you can pulse the mixture in a blender before returning it to your pot. Add ½ teaspoon of salt and the chicken. Set the time for 15 minutes on High pressure.

4. Once the time is up, do a quick release. Add the peas and the cauliflower. Set the time for 2 minutes on High pressure.

5. Do a quick release. Add the coconut milk. Stir well to combine.

6. Garnish the chicken with cilantro. Serve.

Instant Pot Pavbhaji (Vegetable and Bread Curry)

Servings: 4

Ingredients

3 tablespoons cilantro or coriander leaves, finely chopped

1 ½ tablespoons Pavbhaji masala

Lemon juice, optional

¾ cup water

1 tablespoon of red chili powder

Salt to taste

¾ cup carrot, chopped

1 cup of green peas

½ cup cauliflower, cut into florets

2 medium or 2 cups potatoes, peeled and cubed

4 medium tomatoes, chopped

3 cloves garlic

½ medium capsicum (green bell pepper), chopped

1 medium onion, roughly chopped

1 teaspoon of cumin seeds

4 tablespoons butter

For serving:

1 lemon cut into wedges

½ cup onion finely chopped

10 Ladipav bread (you can use burger buns)

Butter for the bread

Directions

1. In a food processor, add the onion, bell pepper, and garlic and pulse until finely chopped. Place the mixture in a bowl. Purée the tomatoes. Set aside.

2. Press Sauté button on your Instant Pot. Add 1 tablespoon of butter.

3. Once the butter melts, add the cumin seeds and allow them to sizzle.

4. Add the onion pepper mixture and cook until the onion softens. Add the tomato purée. Sauté for 3 to 4 minutes.

5. Add the remaining vegetables, red chili powder, salt, and water. Stir to combine.

6. Close the lid. Cancel the Sauté function. Set the time for 6 minutes on the Manual High pressure. Once time is up, do a natural pressure release for 5 minutes and then do a quick release.

7. Open the lid carefully. Add the pavbhaji masala. Select the Sauté mode once again.

8. Use a potato masher to mash the mixture. It should be a bit chunky. Add the butter and allow it to melt. Stir to mix.

9. Add the lemon juice and chopped cilantro. Stir to combine and then turn off the Instant Pot.

10. Serve and enjoy. You can apply butter on the pav (bread) and then toast it. Serve topped with lemon juice and chopped onion, if you wish.

Instant Pot Indian Butter Shrimp

Servings: 4

Ingredients

Sauce:

½ teaspoon of finely grated lime zest

1 cup of heavy cream

1 (28-ounce) can of dried tomatoes, with juice

¼ teaspoon kosher salt

¼ to ½ teaspoon of crushed red pepper flakes

1 ½ teaspoons of grated fresh ginger

2 garlic cloves, grated or minced

2 shallots, minced

4 tablespoons butter, divided

Chopped fresh cilantro

Cooked basmati rice

Marinade:

2 pounds shrimp, peeled and deveined

1 garlic clove, grated or minced

2 teaspoons ground cumin

1 teaspoon freshly grated ginger

1 ½ teaspoons of kosher salt

2 teaspoons lime juice

2 teaspoons of garam masala

2 teaspoons of sweet paprika

¼ cup plain whole-milk yogurt

Directions

1. Add the yogurt, garlic, cumin, ginger, paprika, salt, garam masala, and lime juice into a bowl. Mix well to make the marinade. Stir in the shrimp. Refrigerate for up to 1 hour, if you wish.

2. In the meantime, prepare the sauce. Select the Sauté option on your Instant Pot. Add the 2 tablespoons of butter.

3. Allow the butter to melt and add the shallots. Add a pinch of salt. Cook for 4 to 6 minutes or until golden brown.

4. Add the garlic, ¼ teaspoon of salt, red pepper flakes, and ginger. Stir to combine Cook for 1 to 2 more minutes.

5. Add the tomatoes plus the juice, a pinch of salt and heavy cream and stir well to

combine. Cover the pot and set the time for 8 minutes on High pressure. The valve should be set to Sealing. Once cooking is done, proceed to release the pressure manually and then remove the lid.

6. Press the Sauté mode and then simmer the sauce for 4 to 7 minutes. The sauce should thicken.

7. Add the shrimp and the marinade, stir, and then add the lime zest and 2 tablespoons of butter. Stir well and cook for 2 to 5 minutes. The shrimp should turn pink. You should be careful not to overcook them, as they will still continue cooking in the sauce once you switch off the Instant Pot.

8. Remove. Garnish with cilantro, before serving with rice.

Kadhi (Yogurt and Chickpea Flour Gravy from Gujarat)

Servings: 2 to 4

Ingredients

2 cups of water

½ teaspoon of salt

½ teaspoon of whole cumin seeds

1 teaspoon grated white turmeric, optional

1 teaspoon ground green chilies

1 teaspoon of grated ginger

10 to 15 fresh or dried curry leaves

¼ cup besan (chickpea flour)

1 tablespoon of ghee, butter, or oil

2 tablespoons of cilantro, chopped

Directions

1. In a bowl, add the yogurt, ginger, chickpea flour, chilies, white turmeric, salt, and water. Mix well using a hand blender. You can also whisk the ingredients together, until well incorporated.

2. Press the Sauté mode on your Instant Pot. Wait until the display changes to 'Hot'.

3. Add the ghee to the Instant Pot. Add the cumin seeds. Let the seeds pop. Add the curry leaves.

4. Close the Instant Pot with a glass lid. Cook for 1 minute.

5. Add the yogurt mixture. Mix well to combine.

6. Close the lid well and make sure the vent is turned to the Sealing position. This will prevent the steam from escaping.

7. Press Cancel and then select the Soup option.

8. Set the time for 5 minutes.

9. Once the time is up, let the pressure naturally release. This will take about 10 minutes. Once the 10 minutes are up, proceed to manually release any remaining pressure by carefully opening the vent. Keep in mind that you will be dealing with hot steam. Be careful.

10. Press Cancel and then carefully open the Instant Pot lid.

11. Serve and enjoy.

Shrimp Biryani

Servings: 4

Ingredients

½ cup cilantro for garnish

1 pound Shrimp, thawed if using frozen

2 teaspoons salt

1 teaspoon of garam masala

1 to 2 teaspoon mild red chili powder (or use Kashmiri chili powder)

½ teaspoon turmeric

1 large potato cubed

1 tomato diced

2 cloves or ½ tablespoon of grated garlic

½ tablespoon of ginger, grated

1 large onion, thinly sliced

2 bay leaves

8 to 10 black peppercorn

1 teaspoon of cumin seeds

1 tablespoon of ghee, butter, or oil

2 cups of long grain basmati rice

Directions

1. Rinse your rice and soak it for 20 minutes in 2 cups of water. Once the time is up, drain the rice well. Set aside.

2. Press the Sauté (More) function on your Instant Pot. Wait for the display to read hot and then add the ghee.

3. Add the peppercorn, cumin seeds, and bay leaves. Cook for 30 seconds.

4. Add the onions and stir to mix well. Cover with a glass lid. Cook for 3 to 4 minutes or until the onions are light golden or translucent.

5. Add the tomatoes, garlic, ginger, red chili powder, turmeric, garam masala, potatoes, and salt. Mix everything well to combine.

6. Add the rice, 2 cups of water, and the shrimp. Mix well to incorporate the rice. All the liquids should coat it well.

7. Close the lid and make sure the pressure valve of your Instant Pot is set to Sealing. Select 6 minutes on Manual High pressure.

Once the cooking is done, follow it up with a quick release.

8. Open the lid and garnish the shrimp biryani with cilantro.

9. Serve with lime wedges and hot raita, if you wish.

Sweet Potato Halwa

Servings: 2 to 4

Ingredients

¼ cup sliced or slivered almonds

¼ cup ghee, butter, or oil

½ cup green raisins

4 green cardamoms, gently bruised

½ cup brown sugar

1 cup whole milk

6 medium sized sweet potatoes (around 1 ½ pounds)

1 teaspoon crushed dried rose petals, optional

Directions

1. Peel the sweet potatoes and then cut them into halves. Arrange them at the base of your Instant Pot. Add the milk, brown sugar, and whole cardamoms.

2. Close the pot and set the time for 7 minutes on the Manual option. Once the time is up, do a quick release.

3. Remove the cardamoms. Mash the sweet potatoes. The sweet potatoes should mix well with the milk. Add the raisins. Stir to combine.

4. Press the Sauté mode. Cook for 5 to 6 minutes. Make sure you stir frequently. You should have a smooth thick mass.

5. Add the clarified butter (ghee) and proceed to cook for 4 more minutes.

6. Place the sweet potato halwa in a serving bowl and then garnish it with slivered almonds. Spread rose petals on top, if you wish.

7. Serve the dessert while still warm.

Instant Pot Rice Pudding

Servings: 8

Ingredients

¾ cup raisins

½ teaspoon vanilla extract

2 eggs

½ cup sugar

2 cups whole milk, divided

¼ teaspoon salt

1 ½ cups water

1 cup Arborio rice, rinsed

Directions

1. Add the rice, water, and salt into your Instant Pot, and then stir to combine. Close the Instant Pot lid and then set the time for 3 minutes on High pressure.

2. Once you hear the beep that marks that lapse of the time, give it 10 minutes to release pressure. Next, do a quick release to get rid of any remaining pressure.

3. Open the lid. Add the sugar and 1 ½ cups of milk. Stir well to combine.

4. In a bowl, mix the eggs, vanilla and the remaining ½ cup of milk. Pour the mixture through a strainer and add it to your pot.

5. Press the Sauté function and bring the mixture to a boil. Make sure you stir frequently. Turn off your Instant Pot and the raisins. Stir to combine. The pudding should thicken as it begins to cool. Serve while still warm.

6. Alternatively, you can place it into serving dishes before chilling. You can top with nutmeg, cinnamon, and whipped cream, if you wish. You can also add more milk and cream to adjust the consistency.

7. Enjoy.

Vegetable Masala Subzi

Servings: 4

Ingredients

1/3 cup of green peas, thawed if frozen

¾ teaspoon of salt

3 cups of chopped veggies such as carrots, cauliflower, green beans, zucchini, potatoes, peppers, and cabbage

3 cloves of garlic, minced

1 teaspoon oil

1/3 to ½ teaspoon of cayenne

1/3 to ½ teaspoon of cinnamon

½ teaspoon each ground cumin, coriander, turmeric, mustard

½ teaspoon of black pepper

½ teaspoon fenugreek seeds powder (pulverize the fenugreek seeds and use)

Cilantro and lemon for garnish

Directions

1. In a bowl, mix the spices. Set aside.

2. Press the Sauté function on your Instant Pot. Add the veggies, a bit of water, and some salt. Close the lid and set the time for 1 minute on the Manual setting.

3. Once the time is up, proceed to do a quick release.

4. Add the peas and adjust the salt if needed, stir well to combine. Close the lid and let the ingredients sit for 5 minutes. If you notice that the veggies are not done to your liking, you can cook on the Sauté option for a few more minutes.

5. Remove. Garnish with lemon and cilantro.

6. Serve with flat bread or rice.

Sweet Seviyan Vermicelli

Servings: 2

Ingredients

¼ cup cashews, sliced almonds, raisins

4 to 5 strands saffron or kesar

½ teaspoon cardamom or elaichi powder

1/3 cup sugar

1 cup water

2 tablespoons ghee or unsalted butter

1 cup roasted vermicelli

Directions

1. Select the Sauté mode of your Instant Pot. Wait for the display to say 'hot'. Heat the ghee.

2. Add the dried fruits and the nuts. Cook for 30 seconds. Add the roasted vermicelli. Cook for 30 more seconds. If you do not have roasted vermicelli, you can proceed to roast it for 3 to 4 minutes before adding the nuts.

3. Add the sugar, saffron, cardamom, and water. Stir to combine. Press Cancel and

close the lid. Make sure that the vent is on the Sealing position.

4. Set the time for 1 minute on Manual High pressure.

5. Once the time is up, allow for 5 minutes natural pressure release.

6. Remove and serve.

Instant Pot Idli

Servings: 1

Ingredients

2 cups of water (for steaming)

Oil for greasing plate

1 cup Idli batter (you can find it in Indian grocery stores; follow instructions)

Directions

1. Pour 2 cups of water into your Instant Pot. Put the wire rack inside. Press the Sauté function and allow the water to boil.

2. In the meantime, use a few drops of oil to carefully grease the idli plates. Gently pour the batter into each mold. Carefully place the idli plates in your Instant Pot. Cancel the Sauté mode.

3. Close the lid and place the valve in the venting mode. Switch on the steam mode and then set the time for 12 minutes. You need to check the time, as there is no time display in this mode.

4. Once the 12 minutes are up, carefully remove the idli plates and set them aside for 2 minutes.

5. Once time is up, wet a spoon and then proceed to scoop out the idli.

6. Plate and serve hot with your favorite chutney.

I believe you now have enough recipes to try in your quest towards preparing delicious Indian recipes with an Instant Pot. We won't stop there though; you need to take your cooking to the next level by understanding and appreciating powerful tips that will revolutionize your cooking.

Let's discuss these in the next chapter.

Chapter 9: Instant Pot Tips

The Instant Pot is undoubtedly a revolutionary kitchen appliance that you would want to make the most efficient use of when preparing various meals. To make sure that you make the most use of the appliance, here are some great tips that will come in handy when using the Instant Pot:

1. Use a bit of liquid

It is good to keep in mind that the Instant Pot is still a pressure cooker. It needs to pressurize so that it can cook the food. Where do you get this pressure? Well, you have to add some liquid to your inner pot to generate pressure as the water heats up.

So how much water do you need?

You can add ½ to 1 cup of water or broth or liquid. This liquid will enable your Instant Pot to pressurize. However, keep in mind that water is not the only liquid you can use to cook your food. You can use things such as broth, sauces, milk, and yogurt, depending on the recipe. Actually, liquids such as broth add flavor to your food. Therefore, you shouldn't be shy about using them.

2. Make use of the Sauté function

One function you need to make proper use of is the Sauté or browning function. This function allows you to cook food as you usually do in a pan or skillet. You can brown your food or fry it before you start using the many other methods of cooking.

For example, you can sauté things such as onion or garlic before adding your vegetables or chicken. In other words, the Sauté function basically transforms your Instant Pot into a skillet.

As you use the Sauté function, one thing that will come in handy is a cover for your pot. You can use a glass cover or a stainless steel cover. This way, you can trap the flavors inside the pot as you sauté the food. This will allow the flavors to mesh well. A glass lid has an advantage especially because it effectively enables you to keep a close eye on the food without having to disturb it by opening and closing the lid to check it up.

3. Double your recipes

As you embrace the Instant Pot, you will want to explore various recipes. Unfortunately, great recipes may not be 'large enough' for you and your family. For example, the recipe may call for 2 servings while you want to cook for 4 people.

Well, this should not discourage you from trying out the recipe. Many dishes allow you to double the recipe without increasing the cooking time. All you need to do is to use the necessary 'multiplier' to increase the quantity of various ingredients.

However, caution is required.

You must not overfill the Instant Pot, as doing so may end up clogging the pressure valve. This will cause your Instant Pot to develop excess pressure, which isn't good.

As a rule, only fill your Instant Pot to 2/3 full. In addition, if a recipe has foods that tend to expand as they cook e.g. beans, you should only fill your pot to ½ full. This will give foods such as rice and beans enough room to expand.

4. Explore the pot-in-pot cooking method

When you want to cook two or more dishes, you don't have to cook them one meal after the other. The pot-in-pot cooking method allows you to cook such dishes separately but at the same time.

So how exactly do you go about using the pot-in-pot cooking method? Well, in this method, you put the first dish at the bottom of your Instant Pot and then put a steamer rack on top. The other dish goes on top of the steamer rack; hence, at the end of the cooking time, you will have two separate dishes.

As you use this method, you need to be careful to pair dishes that take roughly the same time to cook. For example, you can pair chicken thighs with a bowl of rice. This way, one dish will not be overcooked or undercooked. They will both be just right.

5. Thin out the liquid

Here's the thing. If the liquid in your Instant Pot is too thick, this may actually end up interfering with your pot's ability to come to pressure. This means that your Instant Pot will not be able to start pressure-cooking. Thus, it is important to thin out whichever liquid you will be using if it happens to be too thick. You can use water or chicken stock to do so. Later on, you can thicken the sauce by adding thickeners like arrowroot starch, cornstarch, and potato starch. Such thickeners can be added once the pressure-cooking is done. Once you add them, you can cook the dish for a few minutes on the

Sauté function to allow the sauce to thicken nicely.

6. Check the pressure valve

As a rule of thumb, always make sure you check the pressure valve before you actually start the cooking process. Make sure that it is set to Sealing. This is very important. Why is that so, you may ask? Well, here is the reason: if you leave it at venting, your Instant Pot will be unable to do its work, because it won't come to pressure. In fact, instead of your food cooking, you'll start hearing a whistling sound to alert you that all is not well.

If you forgot to set the valve properly, simply turn it. This will allow your Instant Pot to come to pressure and your food will start cooking, as it should.

7. Check the sealing ring

The sealing ring is made of silicone. As such, it tends to deform over some time. This is why you need to check it before starting your Instant Pot. It should be seated properly in its place. If you notice something out of order, it may be time to purchase a new sealing ring. In fact, manufacturers recommend that you change the sealing ring once every 18 to 24 months just to be on the safe side.

8. Don't open the Instant Pot on Manual pressure

Once you push that Manual/Pressure option, you need to let the Instant Pot do its work. It will start coming to pressure after 10 seconds. Thus, if you want to stop cooking, you'd want to press Cancel before the 10 seconds are up. Otherwise, if you open the lid once the appliance starts coming to pressure, you will end up with steam hitting your face. That is not a good experience. There is a good reason the lid is difficult to open, once cooking has started. To avoid accidents, always leave your Instant Pot alone and follow the correct procedure when opening it after cooking is done.

9. Know the different pressure release methods

There are usually two ways to release the pressure when you're using the Instant Pot.

The first method is to do a quick release. This method allows the inner pressure to be released quickly and works to prevent overcooking. Ordinarily, the quick release method is often used when cooking seafood or vegetables.

The second method is the natural release method. This allows the pressure in the Instant Pot to be released over some time. This gradual release of pressure works well on foods that have a large volume of liquids. It also works very well on foamy food or foods with high starch content. Whichever method you use, be careful when opening the lid.

10. Practice safety

As you are cooking, it is good to remember that accidents can happen in the kitchen. Pressure-cooking involves hot steam. Therefore, if you are not careful, you may end up being burnt. This is why you must be careful as you open the lid. Hold it like a shield away from you and refrain from looking into the pot immediately you open it. Allow the hot air to escape first every time you open the lid.

11. Deglaze the pot

As you cook certain dishes, you will notice that some brown bits may end up sticking at the bottom of your pot. These bits are not 'spoilt' food. On the contrary, they are quite tasty and flavorful so don't be quick to throw them away.

What then should you do to get them off?

Well, you can scrape them off by adding a bit of water to your pot. Use a wooden spoon to gently scrape them off. This will especially come in handy when you are browning meat.

12. Add 10 to 15 minutes to cooking time

When you are pressure-cooking, it is important to add about 10 to 15 minutes to your total cooking time. This is because your Instant Pot will need 10 minutes to fully come to pressure. Thus, if a recipe states that food should take 20 minutes at High pressure; this means that the total cooking time will be 30 minutes. The additional time is allocated to the time it will take for the Instant Pot to come to pressure.

Your Instant Pot will automatically start counting the time once it comes to pressure. Thus, you don't need to worry about this detail as long as you keep in mind that it will take 10 minutes for the pot to come to pressure.

Conclusion

We have come to the end of the book. Thank you for reading and congratulations for reading until the end.

I truly hope you found the book eye-opening and inspiring on how to transform your cooking with the Instant Pot by preparing delicious Indian meals with the appliance. You have no reason to give excuses how you cannot prepare the different Indian meals because with the Instant Pot, you can prepare meals that would otherwise be prepared using a wide array of appliances.

The truth is the Instant Pot is not just a fancy gadget that you get to use occasionally; rather, it is an effective kitchen appliance that you can use to prepare your everyday meals. So, don't be shy about experimenting with various recipes. You can have fun tweaking the recipes to make them suitable for cooking in your Instant Pot. You can also try out foods you've never had a chance to try out before. So, get your Instant Pot out and use it to make quick and easy recipes for everyday eating.

Finally, if you enjoyed this book, would you be kind enough to leave a review for this book on Amazon, please? I would greatly appreciate receiving your reviews!

I love getting feedback from my customers and reviews on Amazon. Your reviews really DO make a difference. If I get more good reviews, I will be able to publish more books. I read all my reviews and would really appreciate your thoughts.

Go here to leave a review!

https://amzn.to/2NmEXtf

Check Out Our Other Books

Below you'll find some of our other books that are popular on Amazon and Kindle as well.

Go to the link below

ladypannana.com/amazonauthor

If the   links do not work, for whatever reason, you can simply search for these titles on the Amazon website to find them.

Get Our 2 Audio Books for FREE!

Start Your Audible 30-day free trial and get these 2 Absolutely books:

Mediterranean Diet: Mediterranean Cookbook For Beginners, Lose Weight And Get Healthy

ladypannana.com/audiobook

Paleo Diet: Paleo Diet For Beginners, Lose Weight And Get Healthy

ladypannana.com/audiobooks

Check Out Our Other Books on
Amazon

The Mediterranean: Mediterranean Diet for
Beginners to Rapid Weight Loss

**ladypannana.com/books/mediterranean
2**

Ketogenic diet- Ketogenic Crock Pot Cookbook:
Easy and Healthy Ketogenic Diet Recipes for Your
Slow Cooker

ladypannana.com/books/crockpot

Instant Pot Cookbook: Quick and Easy Traditional
Indian Recipes for Everyday Eating

ladypannana.com/books/instantpot2

Paleo Diet: Paleo for Beginners for Rapid Weight
Loss: Lose Up to 30 Pounds in 30 Days

ladypannana.com/books/paleo2

Vegan Slow Cooker Cookbook: Amazing Vegan Diet
Recipes for your Entire Family

**ladypannana.com/books/veganslowco
oker**

Low-Carb Cookbook: Simple and Healthy Low-Carb
Recipes for the Entire Family

ladypannana.com/books/lowcarb

Plant-Based Diet: 4-Week Plant-Based Meal Plan to Get Maximum Benefits from Your Body

ladypannana.com/books/plantbaseddi et

Mediterranean Diet: Mediterranean Cookbook For Beginners, Lose Weight And Get Healthy

ladypannana.com/books/mediter ranean1

Paleo Diet: Paleo Diet For Beginners, Lose Weight And Get Healthy

ladypannana.com/books/paleo1

Intermittent Fasting:The Easiest Way to Eat Whatever You Want, Burn Fat and Build Muscle

ladypannana.com/books/intermittent

PALEO DIET: 100 PALEO RECIPES FOR BEGINNERS TO LOSE WEIGHT AND GET HEALTHY

ladypannana.com/books/paleocookbook

Ketogenic Diet: The Complete Step-by-Step Guide for Beginners to Lose Weight and Get Healthy

ladypannana.com/books/ketodiet

Paleo Diet: Paleo Diet For Beginners, Lose Weight And Get Healthy

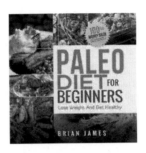

This book has actionable information on how to lose weight and get healthy by following the Paleo diet.

We can all agree that while there are major scientific breakthroughs on various facets of human life, the general population is struggling with some things that they really shouldn't be struggling with. For instance, obesity seems to be a worldwide problem and if the statistics are anything to go by, more and more people seem to be becoming obese or overweight.

Why is that so? Can't we just eat the right foods and avoid the wrong foods?

Well, while there are many theories behind that, there is a striking correlation between obesity and economic development. More precisely, developed nations seem to be struggling more than those that are still developing. What could be the problem?

What's wrong with economic development and industrialization?

Simple: what the masses are consuming. With economic development comes more reliance on store bought ingredients and foods. What you may not know is that these ingredients have gone through genetic engineering, processing and much, much more that changes the original (natural ingredient) to some extent. This is bad for your body as these foods tend to have traces of substances that the body is not yet fully evolved to metabolize effectively. While the body does its best to metabolize some of these, most times the process is not efficient and it leaves behind toxic waste that is harmful for the body in the long term. The accumulation of this toxic waste in the body is what often times causes inflammation and fat accumulation (especially around the belly area). This perhaps explains why our modern society is plagued with so many diseases.

To reverse this toxic buildup that leads to obesity you have to choose a diet containing ingredients in their natural form or as close to their natural form as possible, as this is what the human body evolved for thousands of years to metabolize. This is the crux of the Paleolithic diet and this book will show you exactly what the Paleo diet is all about including:

- How it works

- How it came into being

- The foods you should eat while on the Paleo diet

- Foods you should avoid while on the Paleo diet

- The benefits you stand to derive when you follow the Paleo diet

- How to pair the Paleo diet with exercise

- Mistakes you should avoid while on the diet and much, much more!

By following this book, you will understand how the Paleolithic man was able to remain healthy, agile and fit so that you can model your life like his to stave off various health problems. Let's begin.

The Paleo Diet: A Comprehensive Background

Since this is a beginners' guide, we will start by building a strong understanding of what the diet is all about.

What is it?

The word Paleo diet comes from "Paleolithic Diet," a term used to refer to a dietary lifestyle that is rapidly becoming popular globally. The diet, considered to reflect what our ancestors ate, has been attributed to many benefits. Among them are boosting energy levels, weight loss and healing ailments linked to poor dietary lifestyles. The premise of the diet is simple; if the Paleolithic man didn't eat something, don't eat it either and if he ate something, you are free to eat it as well.

During the caveman's era, our ancestors were thought to only eat game or wild meat, nuts, poultry, seafood and fruits such as berries. Grains and dairy were unheard of during those days, as humans had not yet started practicing agriculture.

Interestingly, the caveman didn't suffer from health problems that we have today like cancer and diabetes. This shows there was something about the Paleolithic way of life that kept these health complications away.

What could that be? Well, while there might be many contributing factors, one of the things that stands out is the fact that food did not go through genetic modification to increase yield.

There was no need for processing to enhance shelf life or add value and there was no need to domesticate animals or practice agriculture since food was in plenty. This means the food was very natural and free from insecticides, pesticides and other harmful chemicals since it existed in nature without the Paleolithic man's interference/input. This worked in his favor, as the body had evolved for hundreds of thousands of years until it was fully capable of utilizing the various components in such foods. As such, the toxic waste I mentioned earlier was nonexistent and as such, weight problems hardly existed.

Agriculture (planting various crops and domestication) didn't start until around 10,000 years ago. This is the time that humans started growing grains and started consuming dairy. Then fast forward to the 1700s and 1800s when the industrial revolution started. This marked the beginning of a series of events that saw more changes being done to food production to increase yield, increase resistance and quicken maturity. The use of pesticides, insecticides, fertilizers, fungicides and other substances increased. And after harvesting, processing of food started taking place. Some substances are now added to food to increase shelf life, to change color, to change taste and any other number of reasons. And since then, the trend has not stopped: we consume more factory-made or modified foods than ever before. And what has been the result? Well, the result has been a wide array of health complications that have plagued our society like never before because our bodies have not yet evolved to a point of fully metabolizing the foods that we eat these days. In fact, our body treats some of these foods as toxins, which explains why we face the health complications that we have these days. The Paleo diet seeks to eliminate the modern foods that are likely to cause various health problems and instead focuses on eating what our Paleolithic ancestors ate. Eliminating foods like refined sugar, dairy, grains, cereals, salt and replacing them with natural foods like grass fed meat, olive oil, nuts, seeds, vegetables and fruits.

Let's take it further by discussing the specific foods you are allowed to eat and those you are not allowed to eat while on the Paleo diet.

Foods to Eat

1. Paleo diet meats

By definition, almost all meats fall in the Paleo diet i.e. game meat, poultry, red meat and white meat. The rule of the thumb is to buy fresh meats rather than those that have been marinated, batter-coated or breaded. Also, choose meat from pastured animals to avoid toxins associated with non-organically raised animals e.g. given antibiotics.

Enjoy organic meats such as:

- Bison (bison jerky, bison sirloin, bison steaks, etc.)

- Buffalo

- Chicken (chicken breast, chicken thighs, chicken wings, eggs, etc.)

- Elk

- Emu

- Goat

- Goose

- Beef (steak, ground beef, New York steak, chuck steak, beef jerky, etc.)

- Kangaroo

- Lamb (lamb chops, lamb rack, etc.)

- Ostrich

- Pheasant

- Pork (bacon, pork chops, pork tenderloin, etc.)

- Poultry

- Quail

- Rabbit

- Rattlesnake

- Turkey

- Turtle

- Veal (lean veal)

- Venison

- Wild boar

2. Paleo diet fish and shellfish

Fish are one of the most important foods in the Paleo diet, and they are packed with great nutrients such as omega 3 fatty acids. The following fish and seafood are top picks for the Paleo diet:

- Bass

- Clams

- Crab

- Crawfish

- Crayfish

- Halibut

- Lobster

- Mackerel

- Mussels

- Oysters

- Red snapper

- Salmon

- Sardines

- Scallops

- Shark

- Shrimp

- Sunfish

- Swordfish

- Tilapia

- Trout

- Tuna

3. Paleo diet oils and fats

Contrary to the common belief that reducing fat intake facilitates weight loss, this has proven not to be the case for a number of reasons. First, fats tend to be very satiating compared to carbohydrates, which means that if you eat them, you won't have the urge to eat as often as if you had eaten carbohydrates. This essentially means you end up consuming less calories. That's not all; eating more fats and oils means that you will effectively eat less carbohydrates. As a result, you reduce your insulin production. Having high levels of insulin hormone in the body has been shown to put the body in a state of fat storage.. In fact, high insulin levels favor a process referred to as glycolysis i.e. fat creation. However, if you eat fewer carbohydrates, you end up producing lower levels of insulin, which in turn helps you to stop storing fats.

The following is a list of some of the best Paleo fats and oils for additional energy when trying to lose weight:

- Avocado oil

- Coconut oil

- Olive oil

4. Veggies

When it comes to veggies, the list is endless. All you need is to choose colored non-starchy veggies such as kales and tomatoes. The rule of the thumb is to eat leafy green veggies and whole fruits rather than starchy veggies, fruit juices and processed salads that contain added sugars. Eat any of these food groups as long as they are organically grown or unprocessed, and contain no added sweeteners or chemicals.

Here are a few you should enjoy:

- Asparagus

- Broccoli

- Brussels sprouts

- Cabbage

- Carrots

- Cauliflower

- Celery

- Collard greens

- Eggplant

- Green onion

- Kale

- Parsley

- Peppers

- Spinach

- Tomatoes

In addition to the above you are also free to eat the following root vegetables:

- Artichokes

- Beets

- Carrots

- Cassava

- Parsnips

- Radish

- Rutabaga

- Sweet potatoes

- Turnips

- Yams

Squashes are also a great addition to the diet:

- Acorn squash

- Buttercup squash

- Butternut squash

- Pumpkin

- Spaghetti squash

- Yellow crookneck squash

- Yellow summer squash

- Zucchini

Mushrooms are also in this category. Therefore, feel free to eat:

- Button mushroom

- Chantarelle mushroom

- Crimini mushroom

- Morel mushroom

- Oyster mushroom

- Porcini mushroom

- Portabello mushroom

- Shiitake mushroom

5. Paleo diet fruits

Fruits are delicious and double up as a source of a wide range of nutrients. However, fruits tend to be rich in fructose, which is still sugar. Therefore, it is advisable to cut back on your fruit intake if you are trying to lose weight on a Paleo diet. That said; feel free to indulge in a serving or two of fruit per day. Here is a list of Paleo-approved fruits:

- Apples

- Avocado

- Bananas

- Blackberries

- Blueberries

- Cantaloupe

- Figs

- Grapes

- Guava

- Lemon

- Lime

- Lychee

- Mango

- Oranges

- Papaya

- Peaches

- Pineapple

- Plums

- Raspberries

- Strawberries

- Tangerines

- Watermelon

6. Paleo diet nuts

These are a good choice for snacks as they contain high quantities of unsaturated fats that are heart-healthy. However, due to being high in calories, you should moderate the intake of nuts to a handful a day. Also, avoid those honey-roasted or candied and heavily salted nuts. You can choose varieties of seeds and nuts from these suggestions:

- Almonds

- Cashews

- Hazelnuts

- Macadamia nuts

- Pecans

- Pine nuts

- Pumpkin seeds

- Sunflower seeds

- Walnuts

Note: Since peanuts are not technically a type of nut, they do not make it onto the Paleo list.

7. Natural spices and herbs

Most Paleo foods do not require added preservatives, and can be stored through traditional methods such as freezing, canning, salting, smoking and fermentation. However if spices are your thing, go for those with no additives such as chili hot peppers, cinnamon and other natural sweeteners.

Here is the full list:

- Basil
- Bay leaves
- Black pepper
- Chilies
- Chives
- Cinnamon
- Cloves
- Coriander (fresh and seeds)
- Cumin
- Dill
- Fennel seeds
- Fresh parsley
- Garlic
- Horseradish
- Hot peppers
- Lavender
- Mint
- Nutmeg

- Nutmeg

- Onions

- Rosemary

- Salt

- Smoked paprika

- Star anise

- Tarragon

- Thyme

- Vanilla

Foods Not to Eat

The following list is a comprehensive collection of all the foods you should try to avoid while on the Paleo diet to lose weight. Chances are you will find it hard to keep yourself from eating these in the beginning, but once you get the hang of it, it becomes much easier.

Moreover, you are also likely to find much better substitutes for these foods.

Dairy

- Cheese

- Cottage cheese

- Cream cheese

- Dairy spreads

- Frozen yogurt

- Ice cream

- Milk (low-fat milk, 2% milk, whole milk, powdered milk, ice milk, etc.)

- Non-fat dairy creamer

- Pudding

- Yogurt

Fruit Juices and Soft Drinks

These are high in sugar and can upset your quest to losing weight, so stay away from them. In fact, soft drinks such as coke are full of high fructose corn syrup and sugar, and are therefore not Paleo friendly. Some of the juices and soft drinks to avoid include:

- Apple juice

- Coke

- Fanta

- Grape juice

- Mango juice

- Monster energy drink

- Mountain Dew

- Orange juice

- Pepsi

- Red bull

- Sprite

- Strawberry juice

Grains

Avoid anything that typically has grains in it. These include rice, wheat, barley and oats along with products that come from them such as crackers, bagels, cereal, pasta, granola bars and bread. Simply avoid every type of food that has grains in it, whether whole-grain, processed grains or whatever kind of grains you come across. Instead, try almond or coconut flour; these are low carb, high fiber, and protein rich.

Here is a list of some grains to avoid:

- Bread

- Cereals

- Corn

- Corn syrup (high-fructose corn syrup)

- Crackers

- Cream of wheat

- English muffins

- Hash browns

- Lasagna

- Oatmeal

- Pancakes

- Pasta

- Sandwiches

- Toast

- Wheat

- Wheat Thins

Legumes

Here are the ones you should stay away from:

Beans

- Adzuki beans

- Black beans

- Broad beans

- Fava beans

- Garbanzo beans

- Green beans

- Horse beans

- Kidney beans

- Lima beans

- Navy beans

- Pinto beans

- Red beans

- String beans

- White beans

Peas

- Black-eyed peas

- Chickpeas

- Snow peas

- Sugar snap peas

Peanuts

- All soybean products and derivatives

- Lentils

- Mesquite

- Miso

- Peanut butter

- Soybeans

- Tofu

Artificial sweeteners

By definition, no artificial sweeteners are included in the Paleo diet. If you want to sweeten your foods, use maple syrup, honey, or Stevia instead.

Fatty meats, snacks, and salty foods

Avoid processed foods, those with too much salt, or other quick snacks that come in a packaged form. For example, if you want to eat meat, just go for some steak, but stay away from these fatty foods:

- Chips

- Cookies

- French fries

- Hot dogs

- Ketchup

- Pastries

- Pretzels

- Wheat Thins

Alcohol

Alcohol is a gluten product and for this reason is not included in the Paleo diet. This includes, but is not limited to:

- Alcohol and mixers

- Beer

- Rum

- Tequila

- Vodka

- Whiskey

The list of foods to eat and those to avoid is undoubtedly long. What you might be wondering is; are there some foods that you should make the center of your diet to derive the most benefits? We will discuss up to 20 foods that you should strive to include in your diet to help you get started.

If you like to find out more about Paleo Diet and learn how to cook tons of tasty and more important healthy recipes, got your 4-Week Meal Plan and 4-Week Work Out Plan you can simply follow the link below and buy it on Amazon:

Go **ladypannana.com/ebooks/paleo1**

to get **an E-Book** version on Amazon

Go **ladypannana.com/books/paleo1**

to get **a Paperback** version on Amazon

Go **ladypannana.com/audiobooks**

to get **an Audio** version on Audible (There are NO recipes)

Mediterranean Diet: Mediterranean Cookbook For Beginners, Lose Weight And Get Healthy

Have you ever thought about changing your unhealthy eating habits but you simply couldn't because you didn't know how? Or have you ever felt like your body has been imprisoned with excessive weight that won't just go away? If your answer to any of the two questions is yes, then today is your lucky day. This is because this book will introduce you to what will be the solution to your weight loss and health issues.

So what is this big solution? Mediterranean diet is what I am talking about. In 2017, the U.S News and World Report rated this diet as the second best die. The reason why it was highly rated is because it has numerous health benefits. Some of them include its ability to prevent diseases like dementia, cancer, diabetes and others, its powerful influence on promoting weight loss and its effectiveness in boosting your overall health. What is also cool about this diet is that you still get to eat delicious food and does not impose strict rules, which makes it quite flexible.

If you are ready to change your life for the better and adopt a healthy lifestyle, then adopting the Mediterranean diet is the best decision you could ever make. Thanks to this book, you will have all the information you need to get started with the book.

Here is a preview of what you will learn:

- What the Mediterranean diet is

- Where it originated from

- How it works

- How it is beneficial to your health

- What to eat in order to reap the health benefits

- What steps you will need to take to adopt it

- Many tasty recipes that you can try

Understanding The Mediterranean Diet

As a beginner you are probably wondering what a Mediterranean diet is. Don't worry, that question is going to be extensively answered in this chapter. But that's not the only thing this chapter will do. It will also try to give you a better understanding of what the Mediterranean is looking at its origins and how it works.

So what is the Mediterranean diet?

The Mediterranean diet is based on the traditional foods that people who lived in the Mediterranean countries like Greece, Spain and Italy used to eat back in 1940s and 1950s. Although the word Mediterranean is accompanied by the word diet, it is not really a diet but rather an eating lifestyle that requires you to eat meals which are high on plant based foods (like legumes, vegetables, seeds, nuts, whole grains and fruits), moderate to high on fish and moderate on dairy products like yogurt and cheese. While on the diet, you can also occasionally drink red wine and red meat or non fish meat products.

That said, the Mediterranean diet is not only about food, it is also about lifestyle. When you are on a Mediterranean diet you are supposed to imitate the lifestyle of the people from the Mediterranean region. This means you should be physically active and practice the art of enjoying the social experience of eating as the diet requires you to adopt a habit of slowing down when eating to take pleasure in each bite you take. It also requires you to share meals with family and friends as much as you possibly can.

Now, it is very important for you to take some time to know where the diet came from before you can jump right into it. So what is its story?

Brief History of the Mediterranean Diet

As the name suggests, the Mediterranean diet originated from the culinary traditions found in the Mediterranean region, more specifically from Italy and Greece.

Hundreds of years ago, the Mediterranean region was the site of ancient and advanced civilization. It hosted different people who included the Persians, Babylonians, Assyrians and Sumerians who settled on the valley of the Nile that stretched on its banks.

Over the years, more people started migrating to the Mediterranean region and soon the Cretans came in and rose to power. They were followed by Phoenicians, learned Greeks and finally the emerging power of Rome. The territory was then divided into East and West. The process of exchanging powers that happened in the past where Phoenicians overturned the Cretans and the Greeks overturned the Phoenicians resulted into a region that had different cultures, religions and beliefs. Slowly by slowly the people in the region integrated and started modifying each other's customs, language and religions.

They also modified their eating habits through their partial integration. Back then, the Greeks practiced agriculture where they farmed and produced vegetables (like mushrooms, chicory, lettuce, mallow and leeks), olives, which they used to make olive oil, and grapes, which they used to make wine. They also identified with bread.

On the other side, the Romans fished and ate plenty of fish. They were huge lovers of fish and sea foods like oysters. They all didn't eat a lot of beef or dairy products because the climate of the region did not favor the upbringing of grazing animals. As the years went by, the Romans, Greeks and other cultures started adopting each other's foods to a point that the Mediterranean region had an almost similar diet.

The discovery of the Mediterranean diet

In 1960s, a nutritionist by the name of Ancel Keys noted that people who lived in the Mediterranean region especially in the mountain of Crete experienced low rates of cancer and heart diseases. He also discovered that these people lived long. Ancel was curious and so he decided to carry out a research that compares the health of the people from the Mediterranean region to the health of the people from other regions like the U.S, Japan and others.

Ancel did what is now known as a seven-nation study. In this study, he examined how different diets from different regions affected the mortality and disease rates of the people in those areas. In his studies, he looked at United States, Netherlands, Italy, Japan, Finland and Greece. After the study was through, Ancel Keys discovered that people who ate foods from the Mediterranean region, which is now known as the Mediterranean diet had the lowest disease and death rates.

In 1975, Ancel Keys and his collaborator who was also his wife Margaret Keys publicized the Mediterranean diet in the U.S. Their effort to make the diet known was not that successful. Not until 1990s when Walter Willet who was from Harvard University school of public health presented the diet to the world.

Over the past few decades, the diet has gained a lot of popularity and it is now considered as one of the healthiest diets on earth. But why is it one of the best diets in the world? The answer lays in the science behind how it works.

How the Mediterranean Diet Works

In the world today, we have numerous diets, which all preach the gospel of weight loss and better health. The truth of the matter is that most of these diets do not actually work and if they do they are not sustainable because they go against how we were built as natural eating beings by imposing starvation on us. That is why a lot of us shut down when the word diet is mentioned.

So is the Mediterranean just another scam that has come? The answer is NO. The Mediterranean diet is quite different from other diets that you may have followed in the past for the purpose of losing weight or improving your health. This is because the Mediterranean diet was first of all never designed for disease prevention or weight loss. It was just an old lifestyle of eating that evolved naturally over the years inspired by the foods that were available in Mediterranean region; and during that period people from outside the region started noticing how healthy the people from the Mediterranean region were. They also discovered how easy it was to lose weight when they tried the diet.

242

In short the Mediterranean diet unlike other diets was discovered after it was seen to have positive effects on people's health and weight and the amazing part is that people followed the diet each and every day comfortably from when they were born to the day that they died. This was mainly because the diet is not restrictive to a point that one cannot keep up with it, as there are no food groups that are completely off limits and you really don't have to track your food intake. That's how great the diet is.

So why does this diet work so well? What is the science behind it?

The science behind the Mediterranean diet is a pretty easy concept. The diet just uses an overall diet approach where it presents you with a combination of powerful foods that are both super nutritious and healthy. Let me break it down for you.

Normally there are those foods that are considered super foods because they have greater significance on your health. A good example of these foods include salmon which contains omega 3 fatty acids that helps you reduce the risk of cardiovascular diseases, Spinach which contains anti-inflammatory and antioxidants properties that help in promoting your vision and your bone health and liver which helps your body lower its cholesterol levels and reduce the risk of diseases like cancers.

Most of the times when we are on our unhealthy conventional diets, we cheat ourselves that we are eating healthy just because we have added one of the aforementioned super foods like salmon in our diet. The truth of the matter is that one addition of the super foods does not make the whole meal healthy. In fact you will hardly get a noticeable healthy benefit when you do so.

The reason why the Mediterranean diet is so healthy and powerful is because it adjusts your whole diet and makes it a huge combination of super foods which are so important for good health. Actually, the secret behind the Mediterranean diet is in what its food adds to your health. As you now know, the diet usually bases its meals on vegetables, fruits, whole grains and healthy fats.

The heart healthy fats like olive oil normally have lower levels of LDL (low density lipoprotein). The lower level of LDL helps reduce the plaque built up in your arteries and cholesterol in your body. When it comes to whole grains, they are high in fiber, which controls your digestion and blood sugar.

The Mediterranean diet also requires you to incorporate fish into your meals at least twice a week and that provides your body with omega 3 fatty acids, which provides your body with the good cholesterol HDL. The fruits and vegetables provide you with valuable antioxidants, which protect your body against diseases such as cancer. That is generally how the Mediterranean diet works.

As you have seen, the Mediterranean diet is healthy and it works. But just to clear any doubt of shadow of whether the diet works or not we are going to look at some of the researches that have been done on Mediterranean diet and see how effective the diet was when it was put to test. Two studies show the Mediterranean diet works perfectly. Here they are:

In 2013, a study was carried out in Spain, which tried to figure out the connection between the Mediterranean diet and cardiovascular health. The study was done by the University of Barcelona. This study involved over 7,000 Spanish participants who were either smokers, diabetic or overweight. The participants were told to adopt the Mediterranean style of eating which consisted of healthy fats like nuts and olive oils for 5 years. Just before the participants reached the 5 years mark, a comprehensive follow up on their health was done and they were seen to have a huge improvement in their health. The improvement was so huge that the study was closed there and then.

This is what the researchers found. The participants who were at high risk of contracting cardiovascular diseases had a risk reduction of up to 30%. This study was later published in the New England journal of medicine where people were shocked at just how beneficial the diet was to their health.

Another study about the Mediterranean diet was published in the British Journal of Nutrition in 2012. The study suggested that the diet had the ability to lower heart disease risk. It attributed this to the decrease of the so called bad cholesterol LDL that comes with following the Mediterranean diet. The study also suggested that there is a link between the Mediterranean diet and a low risk of cancer.

Those two studies prove that the Mediterranean diet works.

If you like to find out more about Mediterranean Diet and learn how to cook tons of tasty and more important healthy recipes, got your Meal Plan you can simply follow the link below and buy it on Amazon:

Go   ladypannana.com/ebook/mediterranean1

to get **an E-Book** version on Amazon

Go

ladypannana.com/books/mediter

ranean1

to get **a Paperback** version on Amazon

Go **ladypannana.com/audiobook**

to get **an Audio** version on Audible (There are NO recipes)

ABOUT THE AUTHOR

The goal of "Lady Pannana" Publishing Company is to provide you with easy-to-cook, authentic, and tasty recipes.

To increase your health, energy, and well-being, Lady Pannana cookbooks bring together the best of international cuisines and teach you how to cook them in the comfort of your own home.

From special diets to international treats, pick up a cookbook today and lose yourself in a whole new world of possibilities.

No mealtime should be boring, so go ahead and treat yourself!

Browse our catalog of titles and don't forget to tell us what you think about our books. We want to create a better experience for our readers. Your voice, your opinion, and your input only serve to ensure that the next time you pick up a Lady Pannana Publishing Title, it will be better than the last!

To find out more about Healthy Cooking and Recipes visit our blog below

Visit Our Blog => ladypannana.com

You can also stay up-to-date with what's going on here by subscribing for free updates, liking Lady Pannana on FaceBook, or following us on Instagram, Twitter etc.

 FaceBook: ladypannana.com/facebook

 Twitter: ladypannana.com/twitter

 Instagram: ladypannana.com/instagram

 Pinterest: ladypannana.com/pinterest

 Tumbler: ladypannana.com/tumblr

 Google+: ladypannana.com/google

 YouTube: ladypannana.com/youtube

LinkedIn: ladypannana.com/linkedin

Visit **our author page** on Amazon to see other work done by Lady Pannana.

ladypannana.com/amazonauthor

If you have any questions or suggestions feel free to contact us at

ladypannana@gmail.com

Thank you for taking the time to read this and we look forward to seeing you on the blog sometime soon!

Cheers,

Lady Pannana

Wait! Before You Continue... Would You Like to Get Healthier, Happier and Enjoy Eating at the Same Time?

Would You Like to Increase Your Overall Well-Being?

If you answered YES, you are not alone. We believe almost everyone wants to have a good body and be healthy by simply start eating clean and diet. Unfortunately, most of us have no idea how to do it. Yes, dieting can work, but starving yourself just leads to frustration and failure. Also, dieting will not help your health! It will just harm you. What we recommend you here it isn't dieting, it is a LIFESTYLE!

Right now, you can get full **FREE access to Low-Carb eBook+Paleo Report to Learn How to Cook Tasty and More Important HEALTHY Recipes,**

so you can easily and quickly start pursuing your goals.

Low - carb eating is something that has become increasingly popular in recent years. It has been linked with a range of health benefits including:

251

- Improved weight loss (even when you're not consciously restricting your calories).
- Improved concentration.
- Increased energy levels.
- Prevention and treatment of various chronic diseases.
- Reduced blood glucose levels (which are particularly beneficial for diabetics).
- Reduced blood pressure.

Free Bonus

Go Here to Get Instant Access

ladypannana.com/freebook

11828679R00145

Printed in Great Britain
by Amazon